A PERSONAL FALL CRUISE GUIDE
TO
EASTERN CANADA
AND
NEW ENGLAND
2022-23

Volume 2 - New England Ports of Call in Full Colour

CONTENTS

INTRODUCTION	3
ABOUT CRUISING	8
THE BIG PICTURE	16
WHERE THINGS ARE	20
THE LAY OF THE LAND	27
CANADIAN AMERICAN HISTORIC DIFFERENCES	32
WHAT MAKES CANADA DIFFERENT FROM THE UNITED STATES	47
THE ROLE OF GOVERNMENT IN EACH COUNTRY	60
THE FORMAT FOR PORTS OF CALL CHAPTERS	68
MAJOR NEW ENGLAND PORTS OF CALL	70
* Portland, Maine	73
* Boston, Massachusetts	91

* New York City, New York	121
LESS FREQUENTED NEW ENGLAND PORTS OF CALL	**147**
* Bar Harbor, Maine	150
* Rockland, Maine	161
* Martha's Vineyard, Massachusetts	169
* Newport, Rhode Island	176
ABOUT THE AUTHOR	**192**

The majority of photos used are the author's own except where a credit is shown. I have traveled extensively through the eastern provinces of Canada and know all areas exceptionally well. And I have also traveled through the New England states dozens of times and am familiar with all of the sites you may plan to visit.

The majority of maps used in this book is from Open Street Map contributors and are so noted for each map. For further information or to use these maps on your mobile device, contact *www.openstreetmap.org* . These maps can be enlarged to provide very localized detail, good to have when you are out touring and wish to have a very accurate guide.

A NOTE ABOUT BLACK AND WHITE VS. COLOR PHOTOS: All of my books are printed by Amazon on a demand basis. This cuts down on potential waste of material, but increases the per unit cost. I therefore offer both a black and white and color edition of each major title. However, the full color edition is relatively costly whereas the black and white edition is priced at a rate more people are willing or capable to spend.

INTRODUCTION

Every year a transformation occurs in the broadleaf forests of eastern Canada and the northeastern United States. It is known as the changing of the colors, and it is one of nature's most breathtaking spectacles. As the days begin to shorten and the nights become colder, the leaves of the deciduous broadleaf trees begin to lose their ability to produce the vital sugars that keep the tree nourished during spring and summer. The trees prepare to become dormant in advance of the long, cold winters. As the leaves begin to die, a physical change occurs in which the chemical composition of each leaf is altered. The end result is an incredible transformation of the leaf color from green to yellow, gold, orange or red, depending upon the particular species. And since the forests are a mix of species, the colors splash across the landscape in a patchwork quilt of daubs of brilliance. Whole hillsides or riverbanks begin to blaze in vivid warm tones, visually dazzling to the human eye. And it is this natural phenomenon that draws visitors from all over the world to bear witness. It begins in the northern reaches of the broadleaf forest where it mixes with the great boreal taiga whose coniferous trees do not shed their needles all at once. By mid-September the first tinges of color were always seen north of the St. Lawrence River in the Canadian Shield or at the higher elevations of the northern Appalachian Mountains of the New England states. Slowly as the calendar progresses, the color change works its way south or lower in elevation until by mid to late October the whole region would generally be ablaze. Like a real fire, the change engulfs every broadleaf tree, joining all their shades of color into a kaleidoscope of hues that brings out the cameras and paintbrushes.

It is important to note that with warming temperatures brought about by climate change, there have been significant changes in the timing and intensity of the fall colors. What was noted above is no longer as reliable a guide to the changing of the colors. Much now depends upon how warm the daytime temperatures are in September and into early October. This will impact both the start of the fall color season and also the intensity of the actual color itself. In 2015, for example, the colors came about two weeks later than normal but were as intense and brilliant as those of us who have lived in these parts can remember. In 2017, exceptionally unseasonable temperatures persisted into early October. Thus the fall color season came late and in many areas it was nowhere near as vibrant as expected, nor did it last as long. Yet in many localized pockets the color was brilliant and even lasted until early November. Once it was so reliable that you could book a tour or cruise in late September or early October and virtually be assured of a dynamic color change. In 2020 the fall colors were quite brilliant and lasted well into the early part of November.

THE BOTTOM LINE TODAY IS TO NOT BOOK A FALL COLOR CRUISE FOR ANY DATE PRIOR TO THE SECOND WEEK OF OCTOBER.

Many cruise lines still have not adjusted their schedules and offer what are promoted to be fall color cruises in early to mid-September. Then if guests on board complain about there being no color change, senior staff offer an apology but do not realize that their company has not altered its fall cruise schedule to accommodate the new reality. If you book such a cruise, no matter the potential discounted price, you will see little or no color. And even booking in early October is no longer an absolute guarantee of brilliant color. Essentially these days it is a gamble as to when and how much color you will see. For this reason I caution you against booking the less expensive September cruises if seeing the changing color is your objective.

Likewise the weather patterns are producing a higher frequency of late season tropical storms that the Jet Stream steers north along the Atlantic Coast. In 2017, there were three such tropical storms that had an impact upon the comfort level while cruising the Atlantic coast between New York and the Gulf of St. Lawrence. In actuality twice in October and early November of that year the storms were strong enough to have been classed as the remains of hurricanes. I experienced one in October of 2017 and as seasoned a travel that I am, I must admit it was both unnerving and very uncomfortable. If you are the least bit susceptible to motion sickness, this is a factor to consider.

With less predictable weather conditions, there also appear to be more days with partial or total cloud cover or even with rain than years ago, still another challenge of a changing climate. But overall, the middle of October still tends to be the best window for maximizing your viewing pleasure. I would be remiss if I had failed to mention these additional challenge to cruising eastern Canada and New England at this time of year. Yet it is still worth the possible risk of less intense color and a few rocky days at sea because if you hit it right, this is one of nature's greatest spectacles. My point is that you need to be prepared for less than perfect conditions. This is a price we are paying for a changing climate. My best advice is to book your cruise for the second half of October to maximize your viewing.

Going back as far as colonial times, locals would ride their carriages or wagons into the countryside and often picnic or camp out just to witness this spectacle, many spending the weekend in communion with nature. By the late 19th century, railroads began to offer special excursions that brought visitors from even greater distances. Country inns that used to cater to spring and summer visitors from the cities began to remain open past the Labor/Labour Day weekend to accommodate those who were now coming to enjoy the fall foliage. Visitors were dubbed "leaf peepers" by locals and this term is still widely used today.

Brilliant colors are found along the Saguenay River in Québec

The cruise industry is one of the younger forms of travel, having taken root in the mid 20th century. People have been crossing the sea for centuries for the purposes of migration, to conduct business and by the late 19th century to travel for pleasure. In the mid 19th century there were attempts at enticing people to travel between selected Mediterranean ports simply for pleasure. One of the earliest travel routes based primarily on traveling for pleasure was between the U. S. Mainland and Hawaii when Matson Lines regularly provided luxurious service to Hawaii. This was soon followed by cruises to the Caribbean Islands. In contrast to ocean liners that simply took passengers across the sea between North America and Europe, and to a lesser degree to Asia, most of the early cruise liners were smaller and of lighter construction because they would not be exposed to the full forces of weather on the open ocean, although travel to Hawaii was definitely a high seas voyage. The idea of cruise holidays was highly popularized in the 1970's by the television program *The Love Boat*. But most people had this notion in mind that a cruise had to be limited to the tropics given that Hawaii and the Caribbean were the more common vacation destinations for cruisers. However, adventure tours by ship to Alaska date back to the 1880's and to Norway in the early 20th century, these definitely not being tropical environments. Today cruises are offered by dozens of companies to almost all parts of the world, including the Amazon River and Antarctica.

Late fall colors in Ville de Quèbec

The idea of fall cruising the St. Lawrence River, around the shores of the Canadian Atlantic provinces and the New England shores came later, and today this is one of the most in demand itineraries with most major cruise lines participating. What easier way to see the cavalcade of brilliant colors without the need to be driving hundreds of miles, staying in numerous hotels or country inns than to do it on board a luxury cruise ship. As more people are introduced to the comfort and convenience of cruising, it has become one of the most sought after means for viewing the changing colors of eastern Canada and New England. Again there is one limitation to a fall cruise to see the colors as opposed to motoring. The limitation is a fact of geography. The richest color is always to be found at higher elevations and more northern latitudes because of the colder temperatures. The moderating influence of the sea inhibits the full glory of the color as well as delaying the onset with regard to timing. When you cruise, it is essential to book shore excursions that are going to travel inland away from the coast, or to arrange your own excursions by rental car, taxi or with a personal driver to enable you to travel either inland or to higher elevations to maximize your fall color viewing.

If you have any wish to book a fall cruise to this part of the world, it is best to initiate a booking at least a year to ten months prior. I have been immersing my senses in the spectacle of fall color change for my entire adult life, and I never lose the thrill of seeing the foliage burst forth in its majestic brilliance. After discovering the ease of cruising, I now prefer this means of exploration. Yes I still rent cars or hire a local taxi, but only in each port, leaving the long distance travel to the ship. This enables me to visit several regions on one trip, something difficult to do by car without exhausting myself. After reading my book, I hope you too will become convinced of the joy of sailing through this spectacular part of the world. But do keep in mind the potentials for disappointment that I have noted so as to not return home sorry you traveled. Even if you only have a few days of perfect weather and brilliant color, it will give you lasting memories.

Dr. Lew Deitch,
January 2021

ABOUT CRUISING

With the popularity of the eastern Canadian and New England fall landscape, almost all of the major cruise lines have made this a buyer's market. There is essentially a cruise for every budget, taste and time frame. This chapter will help you pick the cruise that is right for you.

CRUISE SHIPS: Which cruise operator to choose should be determined by several factors combined. For some travelers price is a dominant factor while for others it is the availability of a great variety of fun-filled activities. Still others consider the degree of luxury, the size and comfort, of the accommodations and the quality of the food. The length of the cruise, the number and nature of the ports of call and the diversity of the excursions is a prime consideration for many prospective passengers. When you combine all these factors, it makes choosing what is right for you somewhat difficult. You cannot have everything in one package, so you must ask yourself what are the most important elements as to which cruise you will choose.

Cruise ship size is measured in terms of the number of passengers they can carry and also by their gross weight displacement. Mega ships generally displace over 100,000 tons of seawater. And they carry anywhere from 2,000 to as many as 5,000 passengers. Large cruise ships are those that displace between 50,000 and 100,000 tons of seawater. And these ships carry between 1,000 and 2,000 passengers. Ships that are smaller than 50,000 tons can hold less than 1,000 passengers, the smallest being less than 30,000 tons and accommodating fewer than 500 passengers. It is safe to say that the smaller cruise ships will offer more luxury and at a higher price, or they will be of the adventure class capable of sailing into very small ports, but again at a higher cost to the passenger.

Ocean liners are in a category all their own, and there are only a handful of mega ships that are truly classed as liners. These ships are built much stronger to be able to handle long ocean journeys where weather conditions can cause the seas to become quite rough. But ocean liners will only do a fall color cruise if it is part of their transition from the Mediterranean or northern European summer season to the Caribbean for the winter. Many do a direct Transatlantic route, but some do travel via Iceland and the Canadian Atlantic Provinces and New England.

Ocean liners offer two to three levels of service from extremely luxurious to basic. Gone are the days when third class, also known as steerage, is where many immigrants travelled during the first half of the 20th century. On the few existing ocean liners, separate dining and lounge facilities are normally provided for the different levels of accommodation, similar to the days when true classes of service existed. These ships generally have fixed itineraries between two major ports, sometimes with ports of call en route. But these ships are also used on occasion for cruise itineraries even though that is not their primary function. Today the most celebrated of the ocean liners are those of Cunard Line, a company whose reputation goes back decades, long before the advent of the cruise ship itself.

The mass-market cruise lines such as Royal Caribbean, Princess, Celebrity, Carnival and Costa to name a few, are normally the ones with the largest ships that can accommodate thousands of guests. And they are the ones that will offer the lowest prices for the more basic cabins, often on lower decks and in many cases without an outside window. They do, however, also have a great range of cabins and price categories, including luxury suites. These ships offer a great variety of restaurants, lounges, and theater performances, on board outdoor activities some of which are quite appealing to younger cruisers such as rock climbing and white water sports. The "glitz and glamour" factor is very important to many cruisers and it is on these "mega" ships that you will find it.

During periods when the sea is somewhat rough, or in truly stormy weather, the larger ships do tend to provide a smoother ride because of their massive size and weight. This becomes an advantage only during such conditions. But on a day-to-day basis, the larger ships are unable to visit many of the smaller ports, which often tend to be very distinctive and special. When a large ship must resort to sending its guests on shore by tender, it becomes a herculean task that is not feasible. Even when docked in the larger ports, guests are simply a part of a massive influx of visitors. It often is time consuming just to disembark and return to the ship when there are thousands of passengers. And on excursions, the cruise lines tend to fill the coaches to capacity, leaving little breathing room.

The bottom line on the mass-market cruise ships is simply the fact that as a guest you are one of thousands, and personalized service is difficult to be accomplished.

Medium size cruise ships, such as those by Azamara, Princess, Norwegian, Holland America and others, still offer many of the public amenities such as multiple dining facilities, large theaters with major theatrical shows and more limited outdoor spaces. These ships will have a wide range of cabins from those with no outside view to luxury suites. But on average, the overall ambiance and amenities are of a higher quality and thus the pricing is going to be greater than the mass-market ships. One very up market cruise line whose ships fall into this size category is Crystal. Their ships, although relatively large, do provide for a far greater degree of luxury comparable to the small cruise ships. But they are limited to the ports they can visit, as the smaller harbors cannot accommodate larger cruise ships.

Medium size cruise ships are also capable of offering a smoother ride during storms or moderately rough seas. But of course no size ship is immune to strong motion during major weather disturbances. In the fall of 2017, two hurricanes were able to reach as far north as Nova Scotia and forced the alteration of the itineraries of even the large cruise ships. The ocean can be quite tempestuous when a major low pressure storm moves into northern waters, and ship captains make every effort to keep their guests safe and comfortable. In fall of 2017, it was necessary to alter itineraries and/or cancel certain ports of call because of two tropical hurricanes that managed to work their way north into Canadian waters.

The medium size ships are also able to either dock or provide tender services in smaller ports that cannot be reached on the mega cruise ships. And this gives the guest a chance to visit ports of call that are quiet and not as well known.

Small cruise ships normally represent the true luxury category in that they provide larger accommodations for smaller numbers of passengers. Their dining and lounge facilities are smaller, more intimate and are noted for their superb and impeccable level of service. And these ships generally are more luxurious and also come at a higher premium with regard to cost. Many of the companies such as Silversea, Seabourn and Regent are all inclusive with no minor charges for beverages, shuttle service or gratuities. And on Regent, all excursions are also included in the price.

These smaller ships can reach into ports of call that are far too small for the large or medium size ships. Thus travel on these ships gives you an opportunity to reach more ports of call that are not overwhelmed by competition from the major mass-market ships. The shore excursions offered by these luxury lines are usually not filled to capacity thus allowing more chance for guests to either mingle or have a measure of privacy on board motor coaches.

At sea, these smaller ships can be subject to a greater feeling of motion, especially true in moderate or rough sea conditions. Many passengers find that they enjoy that sense of motion, experiencing the sea in contrast to the more distant feeling of little or no motion on the larger ships. However, for anyone prone to significant motion sickness, I strongly recommend against the smaller cruise ships.

The last category is that of the adventure cruise ships. These generally displace under 15,000 tons and carry less than 200 passengers. These ships are designed to be able to reach more remote destinations and provide their guests with a greater degree of outdoor adventure. Dining and lounge facilities are smaller, as are guest cabins. Although still providing greater comfort, the aim is to offer itineraries in more out of the way locations such as Antarctica, the Galapagos Islands, the Aleutian Islands, Greenland and other remote locations. I consider the adventure category to be essentially apart from the normal line of cruise ships.

Choosing the type of ship for your cruise is important. For most people the type of ship will be determined by price, itinerary or loyalty to a particular company.

CRUISE ITINERARY: The actual itinerary and length of the cruise are major factors to consider. Often in choosing a particular cruise to eastern Canada and New England, it is a combination of the cruise line, size of ship and itinerary that combine in your final selection.

When looking at the itinerary, you must first consider how many days you wish to be away. Most eastern Canada and New England cruises are between 10 and 14 days, but there are a few that have extended cruises up to 18 days. Many cruise lines vary their southbound and northbound ports of call to entice would be passengers to book two back-to-back cruises and thus extend their time on board and have a chance to visit more ports of call. With the unpredictability of exactly when the fall colors will be at their peak, booking two back to back cruises also extends your window of opportunity to be somewhere along the route at the absolute peak few days of the most breathtaking color.

Will the ship stop in mainly major ports where they may be one among several ships in port at the same time. This can be a disadvantage because of the overcrowding factor. In Québec City I have seen as many as eight ships in port on the same day, making it almost impossible to walk down the historic old town streets or obtain service in a restaurant. It is not possible to choose an itinerary that will not include a port or two where other ships will also be present. But the smaller ships of the up market lines provide for a more mixed itinerary that includes lesser ports of call where the large mega ships and even many of the medium size cruise lines overlook.

The best option for having more of a chance to enjoy the scenery and better appreciate the fall colors is to book on one of the smaller ships because their itineraries include such places as Gaspé, Îles del la Madeleine, Saguenay River and Bar Harbor to name a few. And quite often the smaller ships will offer more daylight hours once into the St. Lawrence River while the larger ships do most of their cruising overnight, which means you miss a lot of the color and beauty of the river.

If you are looking more toward the major ports of call such as Boston, Halifax, Quèbec City and Montrèal then the larger or medium size cruise ships are sure to stop at these ports while excluding the smaller cities or towns . And often the itineraries that concentrate on the major ports of call tend to be shorter in duration, and this does impact the overall cost of the cruise, an important factor for many.

The best compromise for the majority of cruisers is to pick an itinerary that presents a mix of major and lesser ports of call and that averages around 10 days. You must decide if the price factor weighs more heavily or the duration of the cruise. And then within your price point you should try to maximize the variety of the ports of call to be visited.

TIMING: As I have stressed so far, but need to note again, the timing of your cruise will determine how much of the fall color you will see. For many people who live in regions that do have the changing of the leaves, they are often more interested in the historic and cultural aspects of the ports of call in eastern Canada and New England. If fall color is not your objective, than booking earlier in the season, between late August and mid-September will impact overall cost as well as the number of people traveling. With the impact of climate change, now the prime color season tends to be between mid-October and early November, but each year brings its own unique conditions and this time frame can often be disappointing in years when the color change occurs as it did in the past between mid-September and mid-October. Some people believe that they can gauge the fall color season by the prior winter, spring and summer conditions in the year they are traveling. This is absolutely not true other than one factor. If there is a great amount of summer rainfall, the trees will sprout more leaves, giving them fuller canopies. The richer the canopy, the better chance for good color, but the drop in temperature in September and October will still be a major factor in determining color.

Temperatures between late August and mid-September are often mild with highs between 20 and 25 degrees Celsius, or 68 to 76 degrees Fahrenheit, whereas from mid-September to mid-October daytime highs can fluctuate between 10 and 25 degrees Celsius, or 52 to 76 degrees Fahrenheit. By mid-October you are more likely to experience daytime highs between 8 to 15 degrees Celsius, or 46 and 64 degrees Fahrenheit. But it is impossible to be certain because of yearly aberrations brought about by global warming. If I could answer questions as to what the fall will be like in 2021 or 2022, I would become famous.

A large cruise ship tied up in Halifax, Nova Scotia to wait out a 2017 storm

With regard to weather, some years see no hurricanes traveling up into the New England and Atlantic Canada while other years see a number of such storms coming north between mid-September and the end of October. These storms can cause rough seas to where it is necessary to alter ship itineraries and spend more time in sheltered ports. Such was the case during the 2017 season. Fall 2020 also saw two storms that had started as hurricanes pass through Nova Scotia and Newfoundland, but they were not as disruptive as the fall 2017 season when I was lecturing on board a Silversea ship for the entire fall period. One itinerary had to be totally readjusted twice and the final southbound fall itinerary in early November had to be terminated in Halifax with the ship staying in port for 36 hours and then heading straight to New York, cancelling the New England ports entirely. Both instances happened because of very rough seas. Yet the year before, the sea was calm and no adjustments had to be made. In 2020 the pandemic essentially forced the cancellation of the fall color season, which was unfortunate.

I do not mean to present what can appear as discouraging information, but I want my readers to be aware of all the variables that nature offers at this time of year. Guarantees of perfect color, good weather and smooth seas are impossible whereas in other parts of the world the climatic patterns are far more predictable. Simply recognize that to book a fall cruise in eastern Canada and New England, weather conditions are becoming increasingly more erratic. But this said, you might still have a cruise that is simply perfect. I have been cruising these waters for over 20 years and have experienced some of the most glorious conditions.

DOCUMENTATION: For Canadian and American passengers it is necessary to have a valid passport in order to board a cruise ship. No visas are required. For nationals from other countries it will depend upon what passport is carried as to whether a visa will be necessary for either Canada or the United States. It is best to check with your cruise line at the time of booking a cruise to determine whether you will need a visa for either country.

Both Canada and the United States will require that a customs declaration be completed prior to entry. Your cruise line will provide these forms once you are on board the ship. In most cases, immigration officers will conduct face-to-face inspection on board ship while customs is handled when you retrieve your luggage at the final port of debarkation.

The colorful Canadian polymer banknotes

CURRENCY: For purchases while ashore, you will need to have both Canadian and American Dollars. Very few shops or restaurants in Canada will accept American currency, and when in the United States, Canadian currency is not accepted. However, major credit cards are accepted almost everywhere. If you are on a ship that will visit the French island of St. Pierre off the coast of Newfoundland, you will find a need for Euros.

ELECTRICITY: Both Canada and the United States use 110 voltage and most cruise ships also have 110 voltage with compatible plug ins.

MEDICAL INSURANCE: For any emergency medical needs on board ship it is important to check with your local insurance provider to see if you have coverage. American private health insurance or Medicare are not valid in Canada and Canadian provincial insurance programs offer little or no coverage in the United States. It is best for all passengers to have a traveler's medical insurance package.

THE BIG PICTURE

Eastern Canada and the New England states. (© OpenStreetMap contributors)

Canada and the United States are the second and third largest nations in the world respectively with regard to their physical size. Relative to the United States, Canada is not all that much bigger, but we Canadians are proud to proclaim, "We are the world's second largest nation in land area." And we Canadians also tell the world that we are the "First Nation of Hockey," but I will allow sports fans to debate the merits of that claim. In size, Canada is second only to Russia with 9,984,162 square kilometers or 3,855,102 square miles.

If you look at the North American continent, you will notice that it continues to widen as you move north. Thus to cross Canada by road or rail entails a longer journey than crossing the United States. Whitehorse in the Yukon Territory is over 1,260 kilometers or 700 miles farther west than San Francisco while St. John's, Newfoundland is nearly 1,600 kilometers or 1,000 miles farther east than Boston. This greater expanse gives Canada two more time zones than the lower 48 states. There is a cute story that explains that not only to Americans not well versed in Canada, but also to the British. A young British banker is living in Vancouver. He gets an email from his parents, which reads, "Dear Son, your brother is flying over to visit you. His plane will land in St. John's next Saturday morning at 10 AM. Please be there to meet him." He very

promptly writes back, "Dear Mom and Dad, you meet him for me, as you are much closer to the airport." It turns out that St. John's, capital of Newfoundland is approximately 1,600 kilometers or 1,000 miles closer to London than it is to Vancouver.

The United States is far more populous than Canada with its 330,000,000 to Canada's 37,750,000 and the land area is not that much smaller with 9,629,300 square kilometers or 3,718,100 square miles. This means that even including Alaska in the American land area, the country still has ten times more people per square kilometer or square mile than does Canada. I grant you that much of Canada is very far north, experiences brutal winters and would be almost impossible to tame and settle. But within those areas that are equitable, Canada still has a tremendous amount of room in which to grow.

Despite the fact that Canada has so much legroom, most Canadians live in the major cities of the country, the majority of which are less than a day's drive from the American border. Some wise guy American once said. "If the border were not there, most Canadians would be living even farther south and they would all be Americans." He must have been from Florida, as his reference was to the intense cold of the northern winters. And he never took into consideration the history of Canada and the pride that Canadians have in who we are. Even though winter can be brutal, the majority of Canadians loves the land and would not choose to live in the United States, although most do envy people like me who live in Arizona during the winter months. And many do spend winter south of the border in either Florida or Arizona, but that is only an interlude, as most Canadians would not want to live in the United States on a permanent basis. We are two different countries with two distinctly different lifestyles, so for Canadians to live in the United States or for Americans to move to Canada requires quite a major cultural adjustment, surprising as it might seem to most Americans. I took a teaching position in Arizona in 1974 and have remained into retirement because it is hard to relocate after so many decades in one place. But my heart is still Canadian.

Eastern Canada's population is found primarily in the Ontario Peninsula, the valley of the St. Lawrence River and close to the eastern coast of the Atlantic Provinces, leaving vast empty stretches in the interior reaches of Ontario, Québec, Newfoundland and New Brunswick. The New England states, though much smaller in overall area than eastern Canada, have a high population density, especially in the three southern states of Connecticut, Rhode Island and Massachusetts. The three northern states of Vermont, New Hampshire and Maine are actually quite sparsely populated, especially interior Maine, which is more like New Brunswick.

On the Canadian side of the fall itineraries the cruises either begin or terminate in Montréal, which is Canada's second largest city having a metropolitan population of 3,800,000. Montréal is also the world's second largest French speaking city, as the entire province of Québec has maintained its distinctive culture since its founding in 1608. This cultural and linguistic flavor is what gives Canada its linguistic duality. Québec City's metropolitan area contains around 700,000, and the city possesses an even stronger French cultural heritage. Halifax has approximately 400,000, and is the Atlantic metropolis for Canada.

In the New England states, Boston is roughly the same size as Montréal, but there are so many smaller cities with populations between 100,000 and 500,000 dotting the southern three states. On the United States side of the border, the majority of fall cruises either embark from or terminate in New York City, the largest city in the nation and one of the world's great metropolitan centers. Some shorter cruises embark from or terminate in Boston. These are the only two ports in the northeastern United States where such cruises begin or end.

A quiet walk in the woods is how to enjoy the fall colors

In this book you will learn about the natural landscapes, historic and cultural features of all of the ports that are possible for inclusion on your cruise itinerary. For each port I recommend the major and most interesting sights to be seen whether you go out on group excursions offered by the cruise line or strike out independently. The book also provides only my personal recommendations as to fine dining, the best shopping and for the ports of embarkation and termination I recommend what I consider to be the best hotels. This is not a mass-market guidebook similar to Frommer's, Fyodor's or Lonely Planet. It is of a more personal nature based upon my own travels and geographic knowledge of the region. It is designed to enable you to become an informed traveler, but also to be creative in designing your own itineraries for port excursions.

I have been pleased to have received many complimentary reviews of my past editions of this book. Of the few critical reviews I have received in the past, the common theme was that my book was not like the major guides listed above. Some critics claimed I spent too much time on the geography and history of the region and not enough verbiage devoted to such things as walking tours, bicycle excursions and listings of pizza parlors and inexpensive restaurants. The missed the whole point. My intent is for you to learn more about each state or province and the ports of call so that you can make informed decisions to visit those venues that will be of the greatest interest to you. It is so important to have an understanding of the local environment in which port is located and to also learn about the history of each region. The visual landscape that you see is a combination of nature's handiwork and that of the people who settled and created the community. If you simply want to find the best beaches, pizza or cheapest excursions this is not the book for you.

And since this book is oriented to the fall season, I describe those locations where you will have the best colors to savor and to photograph. I do not talk about where to swim or kayak since this is not the season for such activities. And for those cruise passengers who wish to bicycle they usually go on ship sponsored tours where they have a guide, as it is often difficult to disembark and then find bicycles to rent. This is strictly a fall cruise book where outdoor activities are more limited.

WHERE THINGS ARE

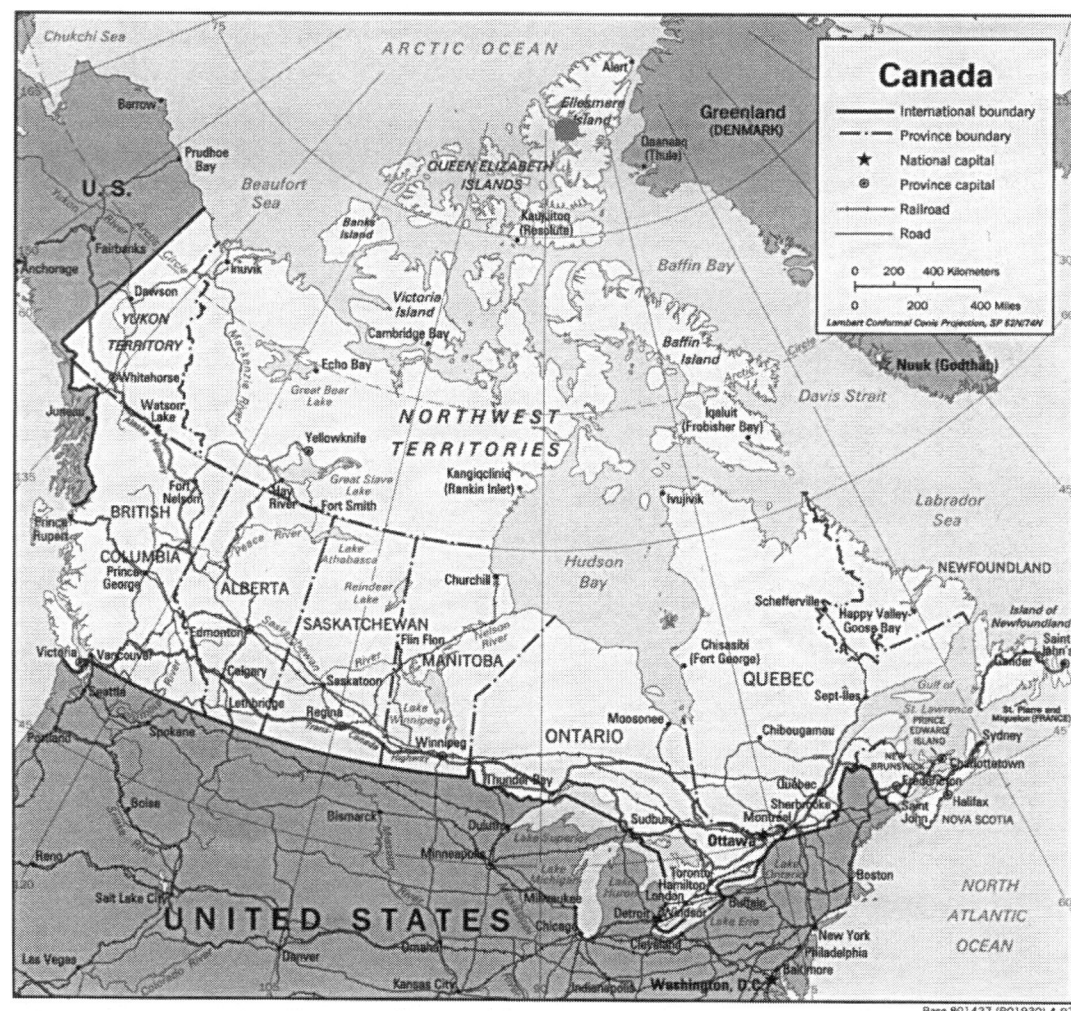

A basic map of Canada

THE WHERE FACTOR IN CANADA: Because Canada is a bilingual nation with both English and French as the official languages, many place names will be difficult for you to remember because they are distinctly French in origin. To appreciate the distinctiveness of Canada, you should become familiar with the map and learn basic distributions so you can see where your cruise will be taking you.

Canada is divided into ten provinces and three federal territories. A Canadian province is like a state, but it has a greater degree of internal autonomy and more political clout than American states. For example, provinces can

negotiate with foreign entities regarding the development of resources; they have a total say in the development of health care programs and they own most of the land within their boundaries whereas in the United States, most land that is not privately owned is federal land. Just as in the United States, a Canadian province has a capital city, issues its own license plates and is well marked with large welcome signs along its borders. Most of the provinces are much larger than their American counterpart states because they are fewer in number. You are lucky in that there are only ten to remember. And yes, you should be able to locate them on a map as well as know what major cities they contain and which cities are capitals. As you read through the book, it will become easier to recognize where places are in the Atlantic Provinces and Quebéc, which is the focus of this book and your future fall cruise.

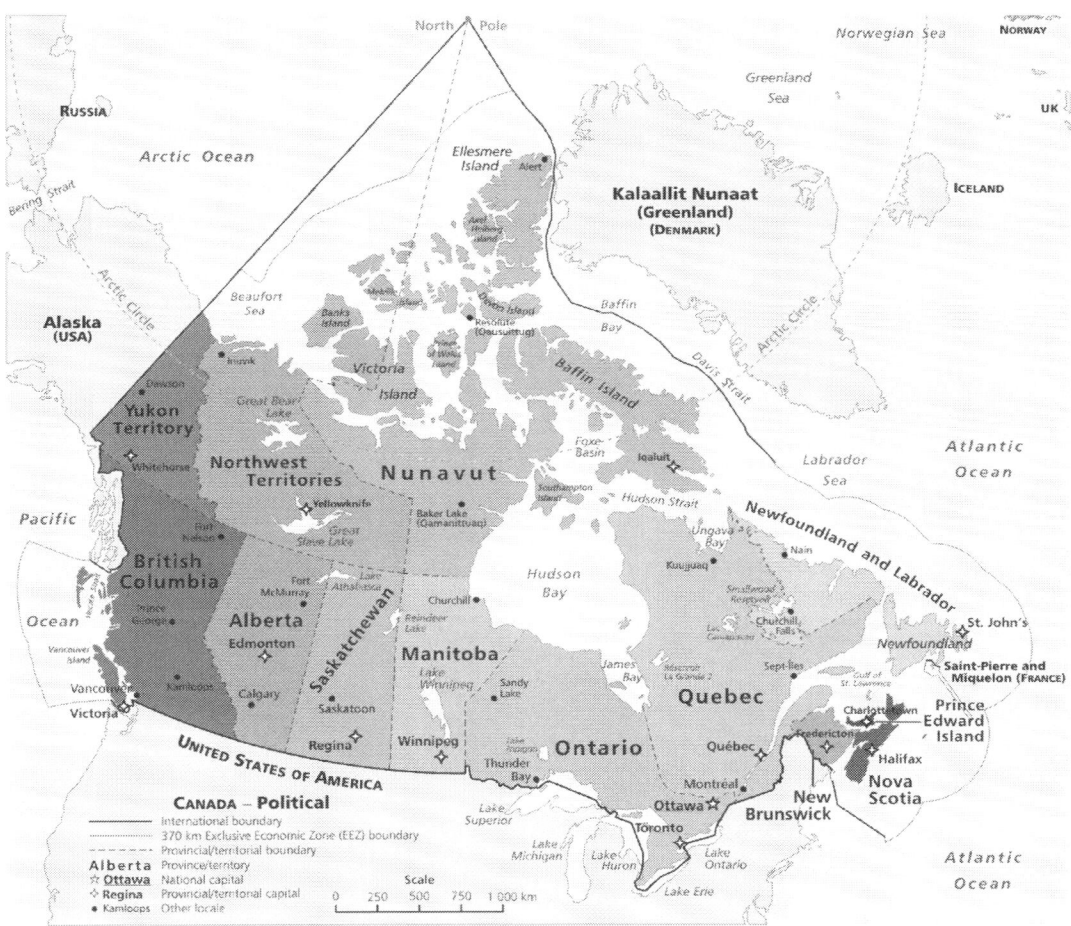

The provinces and territories of Canada

Many who come on a fall cruise visiting eastern Canada and who have not read up on the country quite often ask, "Which city is the national capital?"

Canada's national capital straddles the border between the provinces of Ontario and Quebéc. The main seat of government is in the city of Ottawa, Ontario, however, many important government offices are located across the Ottawa River in the sister city of Hull-Gatineau in the province of Quebéc. As a nation that is bicultural and bilingual, the location of the national capital was deliberate, chosen in 1867 by Her Majesty Queen Victoria to be a center that would bind the two primary cultures together.

Ontario is the most populous province and it contains about 1/3 of the nation's population. Politically this gives Ontario a great degree of power in the national parliament because it has the highest number of seats in both houses, something we will look at later. Quebéc is the second most populous province and it has about 25 percent of the national population. It is the heart of French or Québécois culture, however, there are large concentrations of French speaking Canadians living in northern New Brunswick, Manitoba and Alberta.

The four smallest provinces are those of the Atlantic region where you will be visiting. Both New Brunswick and Nova Scotia are roughly similar in size to the American state of Maine. Newfoundland is also around the same size as Maine when looking at just the island, but Newfoundland also has the large territory of Labrador within its jurisdiction, and Labrador alone is about the size of Arizona. The smallest province in both land area and population is Prince Edward Island, and its relationship to Quebéc on a size comparison would be similar to comparing a combination of Rhode Island and Delaware to Alaska.

Some other tidbits about the where factor in Canada:

* Most of the land area of Canada is drained by rivers north to the Arctic Ocean, thus giving the country two distinct continental divides. In the west, the drainage pattern of rivers is between the Pacific and Arctic. And in the east the rivers drain either to the Atlantic and the Arctic.

* Both Montréal and Vancouver are less than 48 kilometers or 30 miles by highway from the border of the United States, yet culturally they might as well be hundreds of kilometers or miles away.

* Another where factor oddity is that Victoria, capital city of British Columbia is located on a large offshore island that can only be reached by ferryboat, while the bulk of the Newfoundland-Labrador population lives on the island of Newfoundland, again an overnight ferryboat ride from Nova Scotia on the mainland.

* St. John's, Newfoundland is the most easterly city in the Western Hemisphere. By air, it is only a four hour flight from London.

* The territory of Nunavut is the only federal territory administered by its First Nation (Native-American) inhabitants. The territory was created to guarantee democratic rights to the Inuit people, those whose relatives in Alaska are called Eskimo.

THE WHERE FACTOR IN THE UNITED STATES: Essentially the United States is classified by political geographers as a fragmented nation. What this means is that there are parts of the country that are physically isolated and cut off from the rest of the nation by vast distances. And immediately most of you are probably thinking about Hawaii and Alaska.

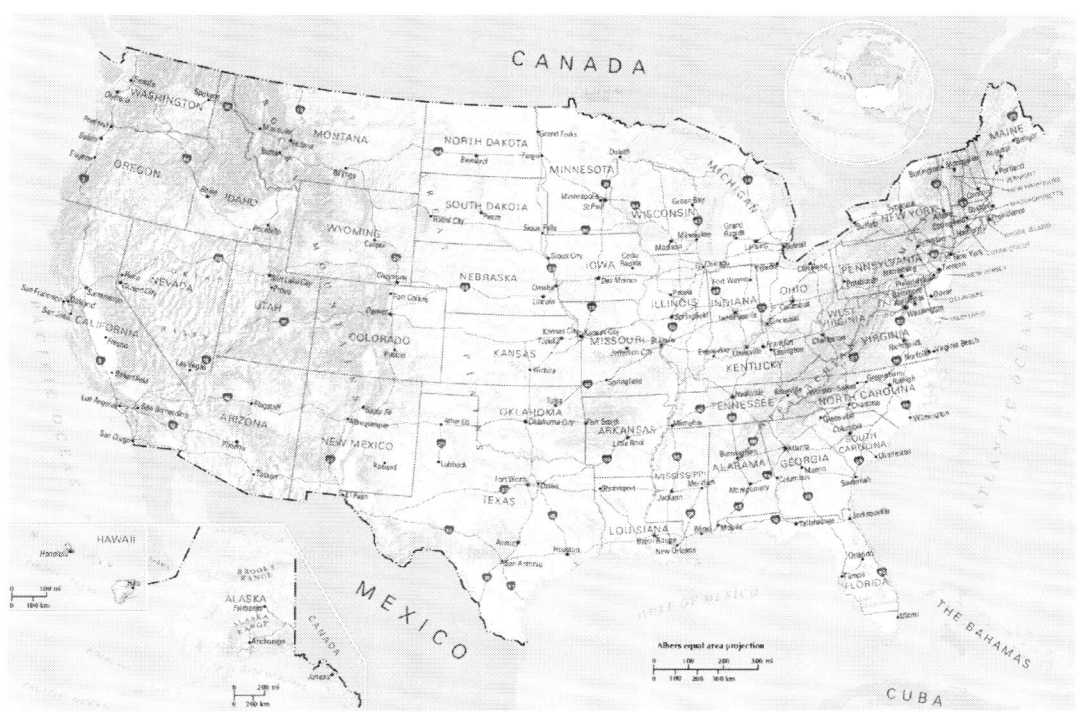

A map of the United States showing each state by name

Hawaii is not even physically or culturally a part of North America. Even that designation of North America has two meanings. Initially it is the continent, extending from the Isthmus of Panama to the Arctic Ocean, and including Greenland. This is based upon the geologic and geographic definition of continental landmasses. Secondly, the term North America is used in a cultural sense to refer to the United States and Canada, two nations with a basic Anglo heritage even though one third of Canadians are French speaking, as France founded Quebéc. But even in Quebéc, the basic legal and political structure is based upon British tradition, as is true throughout all of Canada.

In the United States, Louisiana has a French heritage and the Southwest and Texas were originally part of México and are still inhabited by large numbers of Spanish speakers. The French and Spanish languages are widely spoken in these regions, but they have no official standing as does French in Canada as the second official language of the nation, as guaranteed by the Canadian constitution.

Hawaii is totally different than the mainland. Physically it is a collection of volcanic islands one-third the distance across the Pacific Ocean. It is not part of North America, rather it is part of a vast geographic realm known as Oceania. And culturally its roots are Polynesian with a strong overlay of Asian cultural traditions. What are recognized normally as Americans are actually a distinct minority in the islands that make up Hawaii.

Alaska is of course part of North America both physically and culturally despite its underlying Russian heritage. But to reach Alaska from the lower 48 states requires a journey by road of nearly 3,200 kilometers or 2,000 miles through western Canada, or a sea or air voyage. So to travel overland to or from Alaska necessitates that people carry a passport since they will be traveling much of the route through Canada.

The New England states are the most distinct region within the United States. They are bounded on the north by Canada, on the south by the Atlantic Ocean and on the west only by New York. This was the first area to be successfully settled starting in 1620. And it has retained a strong sense of cultural traditions, a very distinctive architecture, specific cuisine and even a localized accent when speaking. Culturally there are strong relationships between the New England states and the Atlantic Provinces of Canada.

The New Englanders often refer to their region as "Down East" whereas the rest of America calls it "Back East." There are some very distinct differences in the lifestyles of the three upper states from that of the lower, more populous states. Of all the regions in the United States, New England has a more distinctive visual landscape and cultural heritage than the rest of the country. And there are so many visual and cultural relationships to the Atlantic Provinces of Canada.

The people of New England have the most distinctive regional accents of any people in the United States, even including Texas and the Deep South. I personally remember hearing someone in Boston telling a friend, "I sawr you driving your caa yesterday."

Some of the distinct tidbits of geographic knowledge relating to New England include:

* Maine is the most easterly of the lower 48 states. But technically the far western Aleutian Islands of Alaska extend into the Eastern Hemisphere, beyond the 180th degree of longitude. Thus Alaska is the most westerly and the most easterly state in the United States with regard to where in the hemisphere each state is located. This makes for a good trivia question when you ask what is the most westerly state and what is the most easterly state in the United States. Most will answer Alaska for the most westerly and Maine for the most easterly. But in reality, Alaska is the answer for both locations. Food for thought!

* Maine shares its only United States border with New Hampshire, as the rest of the state is surrounded by Canada and the Atlantic Ocean. Only Alaska and Hawaii have no direct land border with the rest of the country.

* New Hampshire is essentially an inland state, but it does have a brief 21 kilometer or 13 mile coastline at Portsmouth.

* With the exception of Maine, the rest of the New England states are among the nine smallest states in land area.

* Rhode Island is the smallest state in the United States with only 3,144 square kilometers or 1,214 square miles.

* Maine has 91,545 square kilometers or 35,385 square miles and this makes it larger than the other five New England states combined.

* Most of Rhode Island is actually a part of the continental mainland, but there is one island in Narragansett called Rhode Island.

* The man made Cape Cod Canal enables most ships to transit between New York City and Boston without the need to sail completely around Cape Cod, saving around 241 kilometers or 150 miles on each voyage.

* There are a handful of farms along the Vermont and New Hampshire borders with Canada where the treaty ending the War of 1812 and solidifying the border caused these properties to be bisected. Thus a few families have farms

that are both in the United States and Canada. And these families must pay a share of property tax to each country.

Sailing on the manmade Cape Cod Canal right through Massachusetts

THE LAY OF THE LAND

The physical landscape is the stage upon which the drama that is culture gets played out. When you cruise between ports, it is easy to lose sight of the nature of the landscape since there is no transition between one port and the next unlike when you travel by rail or auto. Even when flying between two cities, if you are able to see the land below on a clear day, you gain some perspective. But out at sea, even if just offshore, you tend to have less sense of direction and perspective. Thus this chapter will help in setting eastern Canada and New England into better focus with regard to their respective nations.

Yes we know Canada and the United States share many of the same natural landscape features given that they have a long common border. And yes we know it gets colder as we travel north into Canada. But what more is there to know? The landscapes of Canada have a magnitude and panoramic quality that far exceeds what we see in the United States. That may sound like an overstatement, but it is true. The Pacific coastal mountains are more rugged; the Canadian Rockies more majestic, the Prairies show less human alteration and the Great Lakes region has vast areas that are pristine. The Atlantic coastline is very rugged and far less populated than its American counterpart. And the far northern boreal forests are essentially wild and unspoiled. Remember that Canada has only a fraction of the number of people per square kilometer or mile than the United States, and when we factor in that most Canadians live in the major cities, there are vast tracts of emptiness that are no longer seen in the lower United States, but still found in Alaska. The state of Maine continues the rugged and in some places inaccessible coastline south, but by the time it reaches New Hampshire and Massachusetts, it is totally different in character. Here there are several large bays with good anchorage, small sandy offshore islands and the large sand spit known as Cape Cod, which became sites for early colonization.

If one word can be said about Canada and the United States that summarizes the physical landscape that word is "spectacular." But it is fair to say is that in Canada, everything appears to be magnified in size and scope, and this same boldness extends into Alaska. The mountains of both the west and the far northeast of Canada are jagged and most still house permanent glaciers, thus presenting a visual image of staggering power. The vast interior plains extend for over 2,415 kilometers or 1,500 miles as a seemingly endless carpet of grass, dotted with groves of trees and pockmarked by numerous lakes. The far north, which was heavily scoured by glacial ice, presents a landscape of innumerable lakes that will vary in size from that of a small pond to those that resemble inland seas. And almost everywhere, except the sub polar north, Canada is dominated over by trees of the coniferous variety. Along the southeastern margins of the country, however, broadleaf deciduous trees present a blazing kaleidoscope of colorful hues during the brief fall months – an attraction unrivaled in nature. This same landscape spills over into the northeastern United States from the margins of the Great Lakes into the New England states. It also extends south along the Appalachian Mountains, almost as far south at the humid sub tropics of Georgia. And it is that landscape that will be looked at in this chapter with regard to the Atlantic Provinces and the New England states.

A brief description of each of the landscape regions of Atlantic Canada and New England follows, not to bore you with endless detail, but to set before you a visual image of the overall scope and majesty of this part of our continent and to set the stage for taking a fall cruise along the Atlantic coastline, through the Gulf of St. Lawrence and the St. Lawrence River.

THE ST. LAWRENCE RIVER: The mighty St. Lawrence River drains the Great Lakes along with many large tributaries flowing down from the north off the Canadian Shield or up from New York's Adirondack Mountains and the upper New England states. It is a massive river carrying a huge volume of water, one of the world's truly great rivers. As the river flows toward the sea, it ultimately widens until it is over 81 kilometers or 50 miles across, merging with the Gulf of St. Lawrence, an arm of the Atlantic Ocean. The actual fresh water portion of the river is only 500 kilometers or 310 miles long while the Gulf of St. Lawrence is essentially a broad arm of the Atlantic Ocean and it is here that fresh water ultimately mixes with the saline waters of the ocean.

The St. Lawrence and Ottawa River lowlands are among the most fertile regions in eastern Canada. This area is home to millions of residents, primarily within the province of Québec and this valley is where you find the cities of Ottawa, Montréal and Québec City.

THE CANADIAN SHIELD: On the north shore of the St. Lawrence, the land is level in the south around Montréal, but the edge of the hard rock Canadian Shield is only a short distance inland, ultimately edging closer to the river as you proceed north. This is part of a vast region that extends all across northern Canada, a hard rock core of the North American continent exposed by the last great ice age. If your cruise itinerary includes spending a day sailing up the Saguenay River, your ship will actually penetrate into this vast hard rock landscape that is the Canadian Shield.

The north shore lowlands bordering the Shield are covered in mixed broadleaf forest, and the trees ultimately mix with the conifers of the shield as you proceed inland or higher in elevation. It is this mix of species that gives the landscape its breathtaking fall colors that resemble a patchwork quilt of yellows, gold, oranges and reds.

Summer along the St. Lawrence will vary from cool to quite warm, and it is generally humid. Winter is especially cold and quantities of snow will vary, but overall this is a snowy region. Some years such as winter 2015, there was extremely heavy snow, measuring in some areas over seven meters or 22 feet for the season. Fall is generally mild, but with frosty nights. And this is when the fall colors are at their peak, bringing out the "leaf peepers," those of us who come to marvel at the landscape. And of course we spend money, so this is a major season for tourism, hotels, guesthouses and cruise ships accepting bookings up to a year in advance. The only gamble is that we never know exactly when peak color will come, how long it will last and how brilliant it will be. In fall 2015, color came very late, the peak being reached along the St. Lawrence in mid to late October. In 2017, the season came even later than usual, closer to the end of October and because of a warm September, the colors were not as brilliant as visitors expected.

THE APPALACHIANS: The south shore of the St. Lawrence represents a gentler landscape of rolling hills that inland merge with the ridges and valleys of the far northern Appalachian Mountains that extend all the way northeastward from the American South.

Much of Atlantic Canada and New England are geologically a continuation of the Appalachian Mountains, which begin in Alabama and extend over 2,424 kilometers or 1,500 miles northeast into Canada. In Gaspé the gently folded, parallel ranges meet the sea. The mountains continue on the island of Newfoundland as the long ranges of mountains on the province's west coast.

There are numerous parallel ranges of mountains in the Atlantic Provinces that result from gentle uplift of the land over millions of years, but some geologists do not classify most of southern New Brunswick and Nova Scotia as Appalachian. And this also holds true for coastal Maine, eastern Massachusetts, all of Rhode Island and eastern Connecticut. These areas are not mountainous, but rather present a landscape of hills and gently undulating plains with coastal marshes and offshore islands deposited by glacial action at the end of the Pleistocene, what most people call the Ice Age. Yet most maps showing in broad strokes the geological provinces of North America will call the entire area Appalachian.

Peak fall color on the remote Gaspé Peninsula of Québec

This is a maritime environment with cold, blustery winters that produce heavy snows along the coastal margins, and intensify as one moves inland. Summer temperatures are rarely above the 20's Celsius or 70's, Fahrenheit with marine layers producing fog and drizzle for days on end.

The mountains are thickly forested in a mix of both deciduous and coniferous trees, but in many areas stands of pine, spruce and fir predominate. This is a lush habitat for animals, and was one of the earliest hunting grounds for settlers, both for meat and furs. The forested landscape continues right to the Atlantic shoreline where glaciation and erosion have created a fjord-like environment similar to that of British Columbia, however, the fjords are shallow and there are no spectacular high mountains to rise up from the sea.

The state of Maine does exhibit a rugged coastline facing the open Atlantic in what could almost be seen as a fjord landscape, but the mountains are not especially dominant. The Island of Newfoundland is composed of harder rock than the provinces of Nova Scotia and New Brunswick, therefore the tree growth is less dense and much rock is exhibited in a manner similar to that of the Canadian Shield. The coastal margins are also relatively bleak because of the intense gales that blow in off the Atlantic Ocean during the winter months.

SOUTHERN NEW ENGLAND: The coastal regions of Massachusetts, Rhode Island and Connecticut are geologically considered to be part of the greater Appalachian geological province. However, the landscape consists of gentle hills rather than mountains. There are also major bays such as Cape Cod Bay and Narragansett Bay that provide great anchorage for ships and have led to the importance of Boston and Providence as major ports. The land is dotted with hundreds of small glacial lakes and the forests and woodlands are primarily deciduous, thus producing beautiful fall foliage by late October.

CONCLUSION: The picture of Eastern Canada and New England as lands of winter is in good part true. This can be seen not only in the climate and vegetation, but it makes its impact upon the culture. Fall is the best-loved season and in both countries Halloween and Thanksgiving are especially festive holidays. However, Canadian Thanksgiving occurs on the second Monday of October. It is impossible to buy a scenic calendar that does not show brilliant fall colors from this part of the world. And the locals have turned this natural cycle into a profitable tourist industry while still enjoying it.

Eastern Canadians and New Englanders both love and endure the long winters. Winter is a part of living in these areas. Many do yearn for the warmer climes of the south, and those who can afford it often vacation in Florida, Arizona, Bahamas and Bermuda. But at the same time, winter is a part of the spirit of Canada and New England. Think of how many calendar pictures or Christmas cards feature the idyllic valley with its white church steeple and the countryside is draped in snow. Currier and Ives best depicted this landscape for decades. And in places like Vermont, New Hampshire and Québec the annual sugaring when the maple syrup runs at the end of winter is another of those regional traditions that we all have seen portrayed.

CANADIAN-AMERICAN HISTORIC DIFFERENCES

Please bear with me in these next chapters, as they present such valuable information about Eastern Canada and New England that will ultimately make your visit so much more enjoyable and meaningful. But as you read through the material you may not see at the time how this information will be of value. But trust me when I say that it will be most important to your appreciation of Canada and its historic and cultural differences from the United States.

Understanding how Canada and the United States differ culturally is very important to your appreciation of the ports of call you will visit in Québec and the Atlantic Provinces. As much as many Americans may superficially see many similarities in the quality of the lifestyle, many of the same brand name stores and the general living standard, these are not the essence of Canada. As a country it does share much in common with the United States. But likewise, there are many differences. And one of these is their history, which does influence the visual landscape more than you might realize.

I know many of you will think this is the boring part of the book and you will be wondering why it is part of a tour book. Most tour books make the big mistake of leaving out the historic background and then their readers lose sight of what is the real meaning behind the visual landscapes they are seeing. So as a geographer and historian, I always give you a good dose of historic background and many readers have written notes of thanks for preparing them for what they will be seeing. And on occasion, some readers are critical in saying they thought the detail was unnecessary. When I was lecturing for Silversea Cruises, their directors asked for historic detail to be made a part of every destination presentation – a wise cruise line.

Canadian history is quite fascinating because it has many overlaps with the American story, yet at the same time it is quite a tale of its own. The history of any nation tells us much about the present day scene and the cultural makeup of the people. Canada has a rich and colorful history. And in some ways it was the potential threat coming from the United States after its Civil War that helped Canada come together as a nation. It is the history of Canada that gives the nation its distinct qualities and makes it a very different country from its neighbor to the south.

When you visit the various ports of call in Canada you will see important historic sites and architectural features that can only be truly appreciated with an understanding of the events that created the landscapes you are seeing. Thus I consider the historic differences between the two countries vital to having a better understanding of and appreciation for how Canada and the United States differ.

HOW AND WHEN CANADA WAS FOUNDED: The great French captain Jacques Cartier explored much of the St. Lawrence River on his expeditions between 1534 and 1542, looking for a passage through the landmass in hopes of finding a shortcut to eastern Asia. He did establish a settlement called Charlesbourg-Royal on a bluff overlooking the St. Lawrence, but it was abandoned in 1543 because of disease and the perceived hostility of the environment. But all Cartier was hoping to do was sail through the continent by finding the fabled Northwest Passage to China. The rapids that ultimately stopped navigation at what would become Montréal are to this day still called the Lachine Rapids, the name being French for China Rapids.

The French ultimately settled Canada in 1608, 12 years before the Pilgrims landed at Plymouth Rock, but only a year after the British established Jamestown on the coast of Virginia. Ville de Québec was the first colonial settlement, founded by Samuel de Champlain and built on a high bluff overlooking the St. Lawrence River after initial building a small settlement along the water's edge. It is now the oldest and most historic city in Canada. But French colonists were not very willing for the most part to come to New France, as it was a harsh land unlike the milder and more fertile English colonies being established to the south. One had to have a lot of fortitude to brave this new wilderness and carve out a piece of it. And the British were not at all thrilled about having their rival to the north of their new colonies even though the French had come before them.

Montréal was the second major colony established in 1642 that would endure, located at the head of navigation on the St. Lawrence River. The name is a contraction of the two French words for Mount Royal as the settlement was built at the base of a forested mountain on an island in the river from which sentries could watch the entire surrounding countryside for native or British intrusion. So right at the start of its development the potential for conflict was in the air.

From these settlements, French explorers and trappers ventured out into the Great Lakes country and ultimately down the Mississippi River to the Gulf of Mexico, claiming all of the land for King Louis XIV, thus the name Louisiana. Other explorers ventured west into the Prairie as far as the Rocky Mountains by 1748. Although agricultural settlement was limited, and by 1760, there were only 60,000 settlers in Québec, the influence of the French was significant as trappers, known as voyageurs, established regular trade contacts with tribes all across this immense region. Some even lived among the tribes, taking native wives. And the French forged strong bonds with many of the tribes because they showed respect for their ways, and actually copied many of their practices. In James Michener's epic novel *Centennial* about the settlement of Colorado, a French voyageur plays an important role in the early history of what would be the Rocky Mountain State.

The British attempted to box in French colonial holdings by establishing a fur-trading company in the Hudson Bay region in 1670, which became a powerful force that hindered French expansion westward. As an outgrowth of this trading company, Canada's largest retailer, the Hudson's Bay Company, better known as The Bay became the leading department store across the country. You cannot find another department store chain in North America that dates back that far, long before Macy's came along in the United States.

In 1710 the British seized the Atlantic colony of Acadia, ultimately guaranteed by a peace treaty in 1713. As the British gained control of Acadia (present day New Brunswick and Nova Scotia), many of the French colonists were evicted and fled south to the newly established French colony of New Orleans and are known today as Cajun, a corruption of the original name Acadian. The dialect of French spoken in the Bayous of Louisiana is very similar to that spoken in Québec today. When schools in the Bayous want to insure the teaching of Cajun French to their children, they often hire Québécois teachers from Canada.

The French retained control of Cape Breton Island in 1711 and established a large fortress at Louisbourg to protect their access to the St. Lawrence against further British aggression, but ultimately this would only cause more trouble, and it fell to the British in 1758. And the majority of Acadians were then forcibly evicted from Acadia never to return.

During this same period, the British were becoming well established in what would grow to be the 13 Colonies along the Atlantic seaboard. Where the two spheres of influence met in the Appalachian Mountains, both the French and British attempted to ally various native tribes, which ultimately led to conflict over the vast Ohio River territories. Longfellow's famous poem *Evangeline* is set in Nova Scotia at this early time.

THE FRENCH AND INDIAN WAR: Here is one event shared in the history of both the United States and Canada. As tensions ultimately led to war, the result for France was the loss of its most important colony, Québec.

The war lasted from 1754 to 1763, with campaigns being fought from the Ohio River to Cape Breton Island, as well as battles in the Caribbean, North Africa and Europe itself. This was more than just a war for the valley of the St. Lawrence; it was a contest between two great powers over the future control of the interior of North America.

The most noted battle of the war was that over Ville de Québec. Two important generals, Wolfe and Montcalm were pitted against each other in a siege on the fortress of Québec during the fall of 1759, which culminated in a battle on the Plains of Abraham outside of the impregnable fortress. The British managed to draw the French forces out of their stronghold. Neither general lived to see the battle concluded, but the British were the ultimate victors. However, the following spring, the French Canadian militia drew out the British forces and handed them a major defeat. But as a British flotilla of ships arrived in May 1760, the French Canadian forces withdrew to Montréal. But rather than risking another conflict in which innocent civilians would be killed, the governor surrendered on September 8, 1760. Although the British now occupied the two key cities of the St. Lawrence, the war did not end until 1763, when a treaty concluded hostilities.

The Battle for Ville de Québec fought on the Plains of Abraham

The importance of this battle will come to life when you visit Québec City, as the Citadel stands today on the site of the former French fortress and the Plains of Abraham is a grassy park where locals often play football. On special occasions the battle for Québec City is reenacted on the Plains, which delights visitors. Here is an example where the early history still lives. And of course the primary language you will hear and see on all of the signs is French not only in the city, but throughout the province.

The British government inherited a vast colonial territory with over 60,000 French subjects who were now cut off from their homeland. In a gesture of magnanimity the French people were allowed to maintain their language, customs and religion intact without interference from British authorities. Little did the British know what that gesture would mean in the future history of Canada. Had such rights not been granted Canada today would not have its distinct dual cultural and linguistic character. And many sources of tension between the English and French speaking populations would have been avoided. But Canada would not be as distinct and flavorful as it is today. Many of us believe that without the flavor of the Québécois Canada would not be Canada.

To keep from losing their vast Louisiana holdings to the British, France gave control of the territory to Spain, only to later receive the territory back at the time of the American Revolution. The Americans later bought the vast Louisiana Territory in 1803, greatly expanding the size of the nation. Once again you can see that events that took place in Canada would have a profound impact upon the development of the United States. Perhaps Spain had they not given back Louisiana it might never have been sold to the Americans.

THE CREATION OF CANADA AS A NATION: The colony of Québec changed drastically at the time of the American Revolution. Prior to 1776, there were a handful of British subjects living in the St. Lawrence Valley, primarily government officials and soldiers. They did not interact with the French colonists, thus Québec maintained its distinctly French flavor. When the Declaration of Independence was issued and the 13 Colonies began to prepare for war, British Loyalists knew that their lives would be in danger if they remained. A mass exodus of over 40,000 fled to the British held territories to the north, primarily into Nova Scotia, but some 7,000 chose to carve out a new home on the northern shores of Lake Erie and Lake Ontario in the region of Québec that was unsettled. Thus the bicultural seed for Canada was sewn as now there were settlers representing two cultures.

In 1791, the colony of Québec was divided into two separate colonies to enable each culture to exist in its own territory. The English dominated area around the Great Lakes became known as Upper Canada, while Québec was renamed Lower Canada. By the first decade of the 19th century, Upper Canada had a population of over 80,000, most having come from the United States, claiming to be Loyalists, although some were just eager to seek out new lands for settlement.

Conflicts over the border between the new United States and the British along with British harassment of American ships at sea led to the War of 1812, and this worried British officials as much of the population of Upper Canada claimed to be loyal to the Crown, but their pledges had yet to be tested. The war dragged on into 1814 when both sides agreed to a declaration of peace. In actuality, the war was a stalemate as neither side could claim victory. But events left their mark for years to come. We Canadians are often accused of having burned the White House, but it was the British forces that invaded Washington, burning the White House and other government buildings. We are innocent of that deed! In retaliation, American forces burned Fort York (present day Toronto), an event that is still taught in Canadian schools as an act of great audacity.

In 1840, Upper and Lower Canada were unified, an event that turned out to be unsuccessful as the English and French politicians could not agree on issues, literally paralyzing the colonial government. The union was broken in and when the two colonies reemerged, as part of the newly created Canada in 1867, the names Ontario and Québec become recognized.

By 1850, immigration to the Canadian colonies had swelled the population to nearly 2,000,000, primarily from the British Isles, thus English-speaking people began to outnumber the French, despite the higher French Canadian birth rate. Montréal became the primary shipping and manufacturing hub of the colonies, especially since American goods shipped to Britain via Canada could enter the mother country free of duty. This helped to give Canadian merchants an edge, fostering a booming economy. Although Québec was still predominantly French in culture, English-speaking businessmen heavily dominated its economic affairs, a fact that would come to be a source of great tension between the two cultures by the 1950's.

The American Civil War had a drastic impact upon the future of Canada. In 1862, the United States and Britain almost went to war when a Union warship stopped a British vessel to remove two Confederate diplomats en route to London. This so outraged the British that they sent reinforcements to Canada to be prepared for any American retaliation. In 1864, Confederate raiders attacked St. Albans, Vermont via Québec, and despite being later captured by British forces, they were set free to the dismay of American settlers living along the border. Other such incidents only served to inflame public opinion in the United States.

At the end of the Civil War, the economic reciprocity agreement that had existed between the Canadian colonies and the United States was not renewed, primarily as retaliation for Britain's apparent Confederate sympathies. This forced Canadians to begin looking inward and attempt to build upon their own strengths. The difficulty was of course the great distances and the lack of any railway connections to the Pacific. West of the Great Lakes the land was still unsettled across the Prairie. There were minor settlements in British Columbia, but that was thousands of uncharted kilometers or miles away.

In the United States, there had been pre Civil War agitation to fight the British to settle the western border at 54 degrees 40 minutes north latitude, but in 1849, a compromise was reached that set the border at the 49th parallel of latitude from Lake of the Woods to the shores of Puget Sound. Now at the end of the War, there was agitation in the Congress to annex all of Canada, which would have meant a war with the British. But given the fever of "Manifest Destiny," there were many in the American government willing to risk such a war.

The fathers of Canadian Confederation meeting at Charlottetown

Since 1864, representatives of the Canadian colonies had held various meetings on the possibility of creating a federal union. Under the threat of American invasion, the meetings took on greater urgency. At Charlottetown, Prince Edward Island, agreement was reached on a confederation, and in 1867, the British Parliament passed the British North America Act, creating the Dominion of Canada. This was the first time in the history of the British Empire that independence was voluntarily granted to a grouping of colonies. By enabling independence, the British government lessened the threat of a United States takeover. An invasion of a sovereign nation would have brought the Americans condemnation from the world community. Yet back in the 1770's when American colonists were agitating for more freedom the British were so repressive that they brought on the American Revolution in 1776. As a side note, to this day in Britain the American Revolution is called the American War of Insurrection.

The newly formed Canada did not include all of what we see today. Initially, the confederation consisted of only Ontario, Québec, New Brunswick and Nova Scotia. Prince Edward Island, Newfoundland and British Columbia chose to stay apart from the new nation, remaining as British colonies. The three Prairie Provinces had as yet not even come into existence. Thus the vast Prairie region and the west remained in the hands of the British, most of it being administered by the Hudson's Bay Company. It was ironic that with Charlottetown, Prince Edward Island being the city where Canada as a nation was born, the colony refused to join, holding out until 1873. When you visit Charlottetown, which is on most itineraries, Confederation House is one of the most sacred landmarks, it being the birthplace of Canada as a nation.

The Coat of Arms of Canada reflects both the French and British heritage

THE BUILDING OF A MODERN NATION: At the time of Canadian confederation, the west was an empty wilderness containing only

some 15,000 settlers, mainly of mixed blood, combining French and Native American, known as the Métis. The Métis were concentrated primarily along the banks of the Red River in what is today Manitoba. In 1869, Canada purchased the land that is Manitoba from the Hudson's Bay Company for $1,500,000. A later purchase added the entire Hudson's Bay Company territory, extending westward from Manitoba to British Columbia and northward to the shores of the Arctic Ocean. In landmass, these acquisitions made Canada the second largest nation on earth, a title it still holds to this day. The Métis were uncertain as to Canadian intentions, thus they rebelled against the takeover. Under the leadership of Louis Riel, they seized Fort Garry, the Hudson's Bay Company outpost. Their terms for union with Canada were guarantees for protection of the French culture, language and religion, terms that the federal government initially agreed to negotiate. One unfortunate incident in which Riel ordered the execution of a settler of British descent, ultimately forced the Canadian prime minister to send in troops to guarantee public safety during the negotiations. Louis Riel escaped, but the Métis were granted their terms and in 1870, Manitoba joined Canada as a province.

Unlike the Wild West of the American Frontier, the Canadian government negotiated treaties with the Native American tribes of the Prairie and Rocky Mountains, guaranteeing reservations, schools, cash payments and tools in exchange for the vast tracts of land the natives once roamed. To insure law and order in the west as settlers moved out onto the Prairie, the government established the North West Mounted Police in 1873, today better known as the Royal Canadian Mounted Police. By adhering to treaty agreements and through vigilant enforcement of the law by the Mounties, Canada was spared the intense bloodshed that characterized the American expansion into the Great Plains and far western regions. The Mounties earned the respect of Native American and White Men alike for their diligence.

The story of the Prairie is not one of total peace and contentment. The Métis found that Canadians were settling their province from the east, outnumbering them and putting much of the land to the plow so that the buffalo upon which they depended were diminishing. They asked Louis Riel to return from his exile below the border and champion their cause. In addition, many of the native tribes found that reservation life was not to their liking, and conditions were becoming grave as their attempts at farming were met with failure. By the mid 1880's, tensions were high. Unfortunately the federal government was slow to act. In 1885, there were native uprisings along with a major Métis revolt. Federal forces were called in. In May of that year, the Métis revolt was crushed and Louis Riel was captured. Other native uprisings were quickly extinguished, but the government recognized the needs of many of the reservations and attempted to provide necessary aid to thwart further revolts.

Louis Riel, however, was tried and found guilty of treason. He was executed; an act that created tensions in eastern Canada between French and English citizens that would fester for years to come. Today in Manitoba, Louis Riel is regarded as a patriot in a similar manner as John Brown is regarded in the American South. A statue of him is found on the grounds of the Manitoba provincial legislature.

Into the 20th century First Nations Reserves were neglected, a problem that still plagues the Prairie region and other parts of Canada where tribal reserves are found. But today the First Nations are far more organized and vocal in pressing their demands. Old grievances still surface and the federal and provincial governments are called to task by native tribes quite often. It was announced in November 2015 that the homicide rate on First Nations reserves accounts for approximately 23 percent of all murders committed in Canada, and missing and abused women among First Nations is the highest in the nation. This is part of the sad legacy of neglect, a story that has its parallels in the United States. When you visit Canada on your cruise, you will find that both television and newspaper coverage are quite strong on this issue of redress for the wrongs that First Nations people have continued to experience. In the past four years since the hearings that were held on redress, there has been little real progress and many First Nations are still feeling a sense of betrayal. Like in the United States, Canadian First Nations are in essence still unfortunately second class citizens and many reserves are among the poorest places in the nation.

BUILDING A TRANSCONTINENTAL RAILROAD: British Columbia, a colony rich in minerals, timber and fish, was reluctant to join the Canadian confederation, given the distance between the west coast and Manitoba, which was the nearest Canadian province. Their price was a guarantee of a transcontinental railroad. In 1871, British Columbia joined confederation and work began on the building of the Canadian Pacific Railroad. The line opened in 1885, connecting Vancouver with the east. This not only tied the expanding nation together, but it opened up the Prairie for settlement. By 1905, Saskatchewan and Alberta had sufficient population to become provinces. The railroad was built by a private company, but heavily subsidized in land grants and capital by the federal government. In later years, the government itself entered into competition with Canadian Pacific, developing the Canadian National Railway system, which extended a transcontinental line west to Prince Rupert on the northern British Columbia coast, with an additional line southwest to Vancouver. To this day Canada has two major railway companies, one privately owned and one that is a Crown corporation. Passenger rail service today is the purview of Via Rail Canada, another Crown corporation that does a very good job of providing a good network of rail coverage from coast to coast. I have personally traveled coast to coast numerous times and find that Canadian rail service for passengers is a far cut above the level of service offered by Amtrak in the United States.

The last spike in the Canadian Pacific Railway

As a cruise passenger you will most likely not ride a Canadian train unless either before or after your cruise you travel by train between Montréal and Toronto. Many cruise passengers consider a visit to Niagara Falls an important add on to their pre or post cruise itinerary, which is accomplished out of Toronto either by motor coach or train. And rather than traveling by air between the two major cities, they opt for the four-hour rail journey between the two downtown stations. This gives visitors a chance to enjoy more of the countryside. And it is actually more productive time wise than making the trip by air.

THE NATION BECOMES WHOLE: Prince Edward Island, which had hosted the important confederation conference, held out on joining Canada until 1973.
The Prairie Provinces of Saskatchewan and Alberta were created in 1905, as the railroad paved the way for settlements across the vast grasslands. Newfoundland, on the other hand, refused to become a part of Canada,

remaining as a British colony until 1949. After World War II, the British government forced a referendum upon the people of Newfoundland, the end result being union with Canada. To this day, there are people in the province who claim that the British rigged the election in favor of confederation as most Newfoundlanders either wanted to remain as a British colony or gain total independence. Most doubt we will ever know the full truth about the counting of those votes.

CANADIAN AMERICAN DIFFERENCE: You will be surprised at how different Canada is from the United States if you really explore the culture and get to know the people.

A beloved symbol of great national pride

Canada is a constitutional monarchy with a parliamentary system of government. This is completely different than the manner in which the United States is governed. Canada adopted Queen Victoria and her descendants as their own, and today Queen Elizabeth II is Queen of Canada. The queen does not live in Canada, but a Canadian representative is chosen by the Canadian government to serve as the Governor General, the surrogate for the monarch, for a five-year period.

Despite the 1937 Statutes of Westminster granting full autonomy to the Canadian parliament, by choice the Crown is still the titular head of the government. In 1982, the Canadian Government had the physical document of the British North America Act brought to Canada from its prior home in Westminster, seat of British power. The Charter of Freedoms was added under the Constitution Act, and over the ensuing years, several amendments have been made. In combination, the Act, the Charter and the amendments form the Canadian Constitution, but it is not one single document like that of the United States.

The greatest difference historically is that the United States rebelled against the British while Canada evolved within the British sphere of influence. Canada and the United Kingdom formed the basis for the British Commonwealth of Nations in which former colonies voluntarily joined upon achieving

independence. Some adopted the British crown, as did Canada while others have become republics. But all hold together through a common bond of British colonial heritage. The United States totally rejected British rule and created the first modern republic.

It took a second war in 1812 to solidify the position of the United States as being totally divorced from the United Kingdom. Yet today Canada and the United Kingdom are the two closest allies to the United States. And the British Royal Family still captivates the majority of Americans. Queen Elizabeth is much loved in the United States and in many ways is almost a de facto monarch in the hearts and minds of large numbers of the American populace.

You can see how Canada and the United States evolved into completely different nations, interacting in both peaceful and at times hostile ways. But over the years, the bond of friendship has grown to where no other two nations on earth have the mutual closeness and respect for one another as these two countries. At times there are problems in the relationship such as the issues over American imposed tariffs on certain Canadian bulk commodities and the not so popular USMCA that replaced NAFTA at the strong request of former President Trump. Both Canada and the United States know they can always count upon one another despite any differences. In World Wars I and II, both countries sent forces to Europe and experienced heavy losses. Only Canadian forces went to war as soon as the United Kingdom declared war in 1939, whereas in both wars, American forces were not committed until later, after the war had taken a toll in Europe. At the end of World War II, Canada became a charter member of the United Nations and the North Atlantic Treaty Organization, as did the United States.

Canada participated in the Korean conflict between 1951 and 1954, but opposed American involvement in the Vietnam conflict. In fact many young Americans who chose not to serve fled to Canada and were granted political asylum providing they had no other criminal record. This caused much tension between the two governments. And Canada extended diplomatic recognition to Cuba and China, again causing friction with the United States government. But ultimately the United States followed suit with China and only in 2015 did it finally reopen its embassy in Havana, Cuba.

Canada has been a partner with the United States in the late 20th and early 21st century conflicts in the Middle East. And in October 2014, Canadians got their first taste of a terrorist attack, occurring in this instance in both Montréal and in the national capital of Ottawa. At the time this book was revised in late 2020, Canadians have expressed a desire to continue with refugee immigration, primarily from the Middle East, whereas the American government had cut back on its acceptance of refugees. And the former American President attempted to make entry into the country more difficult for people from many Middle Eastern nations. Canadians hope to see that policy changed in 2021 and 2022.

DIFFERENT ASPECTS OF AMERICAN HISTORY: The story of how the United States developed is so markedly different from Canada that at times it is hard to keep in mind that both countries share a common heritage. The American Colonies were settled by the British, and within a few decades saw a steady stream of immigrants from Europe, mainly from what is now Germany along with Ireland and Scotland. Also during the Colonial Era, there was a spirit of individualism that ultimately led to a belief that there was no advantage in remaining under the colonial ties to the Crown. This spirit fomented various uprisings against taxation, lack of a voice in London and the stationing of British troops in populated areas.

By 1776, the tensions culminated in the Declaration of Independence that plunged the original 13 colonies into war with the mother country. And the victory led to a complete severing of ties and the creation of a new nation based upon the principles of populist democracy, creating a republic, the first of its kind since ancient Rome. So while Canada evolved within the sphere of the British Empire and was granted quasi independence as the first Commonwealth nation, maintaining its loyalty to the Crown, the United States broke completely with both the British Parliament and the Crown.

The biggest social difference between the two nations was the issue of slavery. At no time in Canada's colonial history was slavery ever permitted. In fact many Canadians actually helped bring and resettle runaway slaves, especially into the Atlantic Provinces. Where Black people settled, mainly in Nova Scotia, there were a few discriminatory laws attempting to separate the races, but never on the scale of the American South.

In its evolution Canada never saw the aftermath of slavery such as the so called "separate but equal" policies of segregation in the American South that was not broken until the 1960's. And given that economic segregation still exists to some degree in the United States, Canada has never known the extremes of poverty nor the crime that has grown out of such conditions. Yes Afro-Canadians did face some degree of discrimination, especially in Nova Scotia, which had become home for many runaway American slaves. But in no way were Blacks ever oppressed by the system as in the southeastern part of the United States.

In part the War of 1812 was over the matter of the border between eastern Canada and the New England region, ultimately leading to the establishment of that boundary at the conclusion of the conflict. It set the boundary between the two nations from the Atlantic Coast to the Great Lakes.

In the westward expansion of the United States during the period 1836 to 1900, there was an attitude that it was God's will that the country should occupy as much of the continent as possible. This policy was called Manifest Destiny and it almost brought the United States into conflict the British over the northern border, but in 1846 the 49th parallel of latitude was chosen as a compromise from Lake of the Woods to Puget Sound. Mexico was invaded by American forces during the Mexican-American War between 1846 and 1848.

And after the Civil War, it was the fact that Canada was a British collection of colonies and that the British had aided the Confederacy, which led to threats of war to eject Britain from North America. And this in turn in 1867 was one factor to helped in the decision to create Canada as the first British Commonwealth nation. So in many ways, Canada owes its development as a separate nation to American invasion threats.

Thus the history of the two countries is inextricably linked. Many events from the French and Indian War through the War of 1812, the Oregon Compromise of 1846 and the American Civil War are shared by both nations. But since the creation of Canada as a nation in 1867, the two countries have forged a bond of friendship that is stronger than any other bonds between nations. One fact remains as a so-called "bone in the throat" of Canadians. There is little to no teaching of Canadian history or geography in American schools. And the media in the United States rarely cover news stories from Canada. Thus when Americans visit Canada, the have so little knowledge of how the socio political structures of their northern neighbor differ from their own. Yet Canadians are well informed about the happenings south of the border. The vast majority of cruise passengers for the fall itineraries are American. And to simply visit ports of call without an understanding of how the two countries differ leaves you as the passenger very much in the dark about the country you are exploring. So I hope by now you can see that Canada and the United States have their historic differences while at the same time having share many historic events. We should never take Canada for granted, as it is a nation with its own evolution story and distinct personality.

WHAT MAKES CANADA DIFFERENT FROM THE UNITED STATES

Now for the fun part of the book, a look at how life in Canada differs from that of the United States. On the surface, most American visitors to Canada see daily life as very similar to that of their own country. But what they see is very superficial. It takes a deep understanding of the values and customs of Canada to get beyond the veneer of Americana that tends to lead to a belief that Canada and the United States are one. Canada and the United States share one of the world's highest overall standards of living. There are indeed similarities in urban patterns of growth, transportation, use of technology and even patterns of dress and tastes in popular culture that lead one to see a greater similarity than difference between the two nations. But this section is intended to portray the many differences between the two countries, with special emphasis upon the way of life in the province of Québec, Atlantic Canada and the New England states because those are the regions that you will be cruising.

CANADIAN TRADITIONS: There are many distinctly Canadian customs entering into everyday life that illustrate the differences between the ways of life in Canada and the United States, again with a special focus upon Québec and New England. Here are just a few strong examples:

* Canadians consider the drinking of tea to be a significant symbol of their British and general European heritage. Coffee is widely consumed, but tea is still the primary beverage, and is usually served boiling hot and already brewed. In Québec there is more emphasis upon coffee prepared in the French tradition, but tea still has its strong place.

* In the service of a meal, the majority of Canadians still set their tables with a greater degree of Old World flair than Americans. Most Canadian households consider a set of fine china to be an essential element. Department stores and specialty china shops offer a great selection in a variety of price ranges so that most households can afford it.

* Sweetshops, tea and coffee houses and refreshment stands abound in all Canadian cities and towns, both downtown and in neighborhood shopping areas. This aspect of daily life is especially pronounced in Québec, as the French heritage of baking fine pastries and cakes is a part of the lifestyle. But in addition to French style baking, many Québécois recipes have emerged such as a popular dessert known as maple sugar pie. Beaver tails are another sweet pastry that is found throughout eastern Canada while out west the very rich

Nanaimo Bar is Canada's much sweeter and richer answer to the American brownie.

* At a dinner party among more traditional Canadian families, dessert is often not served at the same sitting as the meal. Guests often adjourn into the living room for conversation while the table is cleared, and then reset with fresh service before putting out a variety of fruits and desserts, generally to be served around two hours after the conclusion of the meal.

* Canadians consider it patriotic to display the national maple leaf emblem on backpacks, sweatshirts, briefcases or other personal items. Depicting the maple leaf and the national colors of red and white on billboards, holiday decorations or other displays is not viewed as a desecration of the country's symbol, but rather as a show of patriotism. In Québec for decades during the era of strong separatist feelings, displaying even the Canadian flag was seen by many as an insult to Québec, but that is no longer the case. Rather the blue and white fleur de lies flag of the province was substituted for the national flag. Today both are widely displayed with equal pride.

* Remembrance Day, which is Veteran's Day in the United States, is a major Canadian show of national spirit. The wearing of the red poppy in early November leading up to the eleventh day is a very strong show of Canadian national pride and recognition of the sacrifices made in times of war. And ceremonies held at war memorials on November 11th bring out large audiences. The largest ceremony is at the war memorial in Ottawa very close to Parliament Hill can bring out tens of thousands each year.

NEW ENGLAND CUSTOMS: New England is more akin to Canada in its social values than any other part of the United States. In New England you may be surprised to see that many of the same traditions stated above would not be uncommon, and of course there are distinctive local traditions unique to this part of the United States. Here are just a few distinctive New England traditions:

* Hard work and rather Puritanical spiritual values once dominated the original colonists, but were diluted in the lower New England states by the massive influx of immigrants. However, in Maine, New Hampshire and Vermont traces of this rather straight-laced Puritanical ideal still is the backbone of life in many of the small towns.

* New Englanders have a strong love of literature, especially that which portrays life in the region. Such famous American authors as Ralph Waldo

Emerson, Henry David Thoreau, Henry Wadsworth Longfellow, Edgar Allan Poe, Mark Twain Eugene O'Neill, Herman Melville, Robert Frost and more recently Stephen King are all native sons and daughters of New England. Quite an impressive list for such a small region!

* A proud tradition of citizen militias that trained on a public piece of ground called the commons led to New England towns and cities often having a central park called the commons, most prominent in Boston. Today the commons is a source of pride to many New England communities.

* Knitting, quilting and rug making - These are strong traits of the rural areas of New England, less dominant today, but still kept alive in small communities. It is also a major source of income through tourism.

* New England cuisine - Of all the regions in the United States, New England has the most distinctive cuisine, and the sea heavily influences the recipes. Lobster bakes, clam chowder or seafood chowder are typical. Baked cod, scrod or haddock are popular. For dessert New Englanders favored gingerbread, pumpkin pie and bread pudding along with egg custard. And New Englanders have the highest consumption of ice cream per capita in the country.

* Furniture - The simplistic style of furniture of early colonial New England slowly evolved into a style of wood furniture that is today called New England or Colonial. Today companies like Ethan Allen typify the tastes of rural New England.

THE CANADIAN - NEW ENGLAND LANGUAGES: Fortunately for Americans, the use of the English language in Canada is not that different from that of the United States. Unlike Australian English, the Canadian version has only a few minor variations from the American version. There are some differences in both vocabulary and pronunciation. The most common give away that somebody is Canadian is by his or her use of the term, "eh" either as a statement of emphasis or as a question. For example, a Canadian might say, "Nice day today, eh?" Also there is a measure of distinctness to such words as "out" and "again" that has a slight hint of the British intonation. But there are some real puzzling terms for Americans such as broadlooms (carpeting), Chesterfield (couch), concession (country road), garburetor (garbage disposal), Hoover (the act of vacuuming), Loonie (dollar coin) and serviette (napkin) to name just a few.

In New England there is a very distinctive accent, somewhat modified from colonial English. The long and flat sound to the letter "a" is typical such as saying car to sound like "caar." or there is the adding of the letter "r" where it does not belong, for example I "sawr" you rather than I saw you. Some distinctive New England words in daily use include; ayuh (yes), frappe (milk shake), hosey (to take sides), necessary (rest room), packie (liquor store) and tonic (soft drink).

Then there is the matter of spelling. Canada uses the British format in spelling, which can be frustrating for Americans. A few examples are: colour, defence, favourite, harbour and plateaux.

The French spoken by French-Canadians across the nation differs significantly from the French spoken in France. Essentially, Canadian French is rooted in the colonial heritage and has many expressions not found in France. In addition, pronunciations differ from those of France. It is referred to as Québécois rather than French among those who speak French. For most visitors it is impossible for them to tell the difference. Visually it is very clear that French dominates, as by law in Québec, all official signs are written in French only. And shops and restaurants can have signs in English, but they must be by law accompanied by signs in French with the letters two times larger than those in English or the store can be fined.

French rules in the province of Québec

CANADIAN-AMERICAN HOLIDAYS: Like the United States, Canada celebrates New Year's Day, Labour Day (notice the Canadian spelling) and Christmas as public holidays. In addition, there are many holidays apart from those recognized in the United States. Queen Victoria's birthday, known as Victoria Day is celebrated on the third Monday of May. The Province of Québec has its own holiday known as Fête de la St-Jean Baptiste, held on the 24th of June. Although it is a holiday throughout the French-speaking world, the people of Québec have made it one and the same with their separatist movement. Thanksgiving is celebrated on the second Monday of October, and it is a festival of the harvest and has nothing to do with the Pilgrims. The entire weekend is devoted to dining and/or enjoying the fall colors in the countryside. Remembrance Day is a time for honoring war heroes and veterans, and it is the same day (November 11th) that Americans call Veteran's Day, but it is far more meaningful in Canada and celebrations draw large crowds. On the day following Christmas, Canada celebrates Boxing Day, a tradition that goes back to Britain and is honored in most commonwealth nations.

SPORTING EVENTS: Canada is synonymous with hockey. It is the country's claim to fame, but to Canadians it is a national event. Little children can be seen with their hockey sticks walking to the nearest ice rink or frozen pond from as young as age five. On Monday night the majority of Canadians tune in to CBC television for a televised game on what is called "Hockey Night in Canada." In addition to hockey, Canadians also take an interest in lacrosse, a game originally played by the Native American tribes of eastern Canada. During winter, curling is another popular game and curling rinks can be found all across the country. Canadian football is based upon the American game, but with a variety of minor differences such as the field consisting of 110 yards, this despite the fact that Canada has officially been on the metric system since the early 1970's. Baseball and basketball at the professional level have only been able to take root in Toronto with its diverse multi-ethnic population.

Outdoor activities such as fishing, hiking and hunting are popular among both urban and rural residents, but this is also true today for millions of Americans. As a show of the popularity of the great outdoors, it is important to note the development of the Trans-Canada Trail. A private non-profit organization has sponsored donations for the construction of a series of interconnected hiking trails that span the nation from the Atlantic to the Pacific, with a branch to the Arctic shore. When completed, this will be the largest such trail system in the world. All along its length, there are pavilions in which plaques honor contributors, with many names being inscribed in memory of departed loved ones. This has been a popular way of remembering a family member or friend, as I did for my late mother who a proud Canadian who loved the idyllic countryside.

New Englanders are exceptionally fond of basketball, perhaps because it is an indoor sport that can be played during their long, cold winters. Hockey is also very popular, but more as a spectator sport rather than being a national pastime as it is in Canada. Baseball is also a major spectator sport, yet New England only has one major league team representing Boston. Football is a popular university spectator sport and with many New England universities being located in smaller cities, it does bring large numbers of spectators out during the fall season. If there is one popular activity during summer, I would have to say it is sailing. With a long coastline, most people living along or very near the coast and with the proper wind conditions, sailing is a passion for many in New England. The famous sailing race, the Americas Cup, has historically been held off Newport, Rhode Island more than any other venue.

CANADIAN-AMERICAN CITIES: It is unfortunate that I need to say that unlike their American counterparts, Canadian cities are far cleaner, more vibrant and safer. Urban blight and decay are not the ongoing problem that most larger American urban centers continue to contend with, though great strides have been made in many cities to ameliorate such conditions. This difference begs an answer as to why. It is not easy to answer without a major discourse so here is the short version. Essentially Canadian cities owe their greater success to the fact that people have not abandoned the inner city. In the United States, especially after World War II, the flight to the suburbs left the inner cities to those on the lower income levels. As years turned into decades, the inner city died, leaving blight, high crime and downtown became a place where banks and government buildings became surrounded by urban decay. This never happened in Canada. In the United States there is a vast disparity between rich and poor whereas in Canada there is a lower percentage of those living below the poverty level. In Canadian cities there were beautiful residential neighborhoods surrounding the downtown core, and despite many young families moving to the suburbs, others stayed and maintained the neighborhoods. In the past few decades, as more professionals choose not to commute, downtown residential proximity has meant a great upsurge in real estate and rental values and a large building boom in residential housing. And with more affluent people living in the city center, the downtown core remained alive and well. In the United States, apart from Manhattan, the trend toward professionals living in or close to downtown is only now becoming more of a reality, somewhat revitalizing urban centers in many cities.

The downtown core of Canadian cities is the center of economic and social life. Flight to the suburbs did not have to mean an abandonment of the inner city, and Canada is proof of that fact. The downtown of any Canadian city is a mix of high-rise office buildings, major hotels, large department stores, theatres, concert halls, restaurants and museums. It is the place to go for retail services and entertainment. In Montréal there is the famous Underground City, a network of subterranean shopping malls all interconnected with major office towers and hotels. In winter one can remain underground and find every major product and service needed. This same pattern is found in Toronto on even a larger scale, known as "The Path," and it is developing in other Canadian cities as well.

High rise condos and apartments in Montréal on the slopes of Mt. Royal

And the downtown area in Canadian cities has sprouted large high-rise apartments and condominiums that rent or sell for prices not seen in the United States save for New York City. The inner city skyline in Canadian cities is exceptionally impressive, most notably in Toronto and Vancouver, but also in every other city across the country. Adding to the ability of Canadian downtowns to prosper is the provision of fast and efficient public transportation. The major cities of Toronto, Montréal, Ottawa, Vancouver,

Edmonton and Calgary all possess subway, light rail and/or commuter train service into the downtown core. In all other cities, busses and electric trolleys connect downtown with the rest of the city. There is a vibrant quality to downtown. The Hudson's Bay Company store is the standard anchor, and other retail establishments either line a pedestrian only street or are clustered together in chic central city shopping malls. There are gourmet food shops, bakeries and coffee houses. Restaurants and bistros abound. There are first run movie theaters, nightclubs and discos. Fine museums and galleries are found in all major urban centers.

Sports facilities are also part of the inner city equation. You may say, "This is true to American cities." Yes it is true to many large American cities in part. But ask yourself if all of what I noted above applies to many American cities and if there are tens to hundreds of thousands of affluent people living downtown in large, fashionable high-rises. Unfortunately the answer would be no.

Montréal, Québec City and Halifax are the three major Canadian cities you will visit on a fall cruise. Each is very dynamic and all three have exciting downtown cores filled with historic sites, excellent restaurants and shopping venues. And in each city, you will find major high-rise apartment and condominium developments in and immediately adjacent to the downtown core along with old residential neighborhoods that still maintain their original integrity. You will be able to contrast this pattern of urban development with Boston, the one major American city on almost all fall cruise itineraries. Downtown Boston shows a degree of dynamic development, but it is not immediately adjacent to high valued residential developments as is true in the Canadian counterparts.

Boston and Portland, Maine are the only major American cities you will visit in the New England states. Surprisingly each does have an active downtown core, atypical for most of the United States. However, in both cities you will find a limited number of upmarket stores in the city center. Boston does have the old line Back Bay neighborhood adjacent to the city center on the southwestern margin, which still maintains a high degree of elegance. However, there are very few high-rise residential structures in contrast to what is seen in Montréal. Halifax and Portland are of similar size, but Portland has a handful of older high-rises in its downtown core in contrast to Halifax with its impressive skyline of new apartment blocks and condominiums in and surrounding downtown. Halifax is one of the fastest growing cities in Atlantic Canada and is becoming an impressive city for its overall size.

The ethnic flavor of Haymarket Square in downtown Boston

TRANSPORTATION SERVICES: All Canadian cities provide excellent public bus or trolley bus service. Toronto, Montréal and Vancouver are large enough to have an efficient Metro and double deck commuter rail service to their outer suburbs.

There are two railroads operating in the country, Canadian National and Canadian Pacific, often providing parallel routes, but a Crown Corporation known as Via Rail Canada now provides all passenger service. Unlike the American Amtrak, Via Rail provides outstanding service and is well patronized. Trains are modern, exceptionally clean and offer both standard and Via One (first class) services. From Montréal to Halifax there is the Ocean Limited, a modern overnight train providing both economic coach and first class sleeping car services. First class passengers have their own dining and lounge car facilities. The Corridor is the busiest passenger rail sector of the country with multiple services between Windsor or Port Huron and Toronto, Niagara Falls and Toronto, Ottawa and Toronto, Montréal and Toronto, Montréal and Québec City and between Ottawa and Montréal. Those traveling in Via One class have full meals prepared and served to them at their seats.

Ferryboats provide overnight service to Newfoundland with sleeping accommodation for those who wish to pay for the upgrade. Local ferry boat services cross the St. Lawrence and Saguenay Rivers where needed, and there is still ferry service to Prince Edward Island even though the new bridge links the island and mainland.

Air Canada and West Jet offer service nationwide with smaller airlines and feeder lines serving more remote locations. Air Canada and West Jet also offer international service and Air Canada is ranked by travel sources as being among the world's 20 best airlines. In recent years, it has been ranked as the best airline for passenger service in North America. It offers many flights between major Canadian cities and the United States both through its regular Air Canada and its Air Canada Rouge services. Montréal, Halifax and St. John's, Newfoundland all have direct air service to the United Kingdom, and Toronto and Montréal are linked to many more European and world cities. And many western Canadian cities such as Vancouver, Calgary and Edmonton have transoceanic service to cities in Europe, the Caribbean and Asia.

The Toronto subway system is spotless, as is the Montréal Metro

Public transport in small American cities is often not on an equal footing with similar size Canadian cities. However, Portland, Maine does have as good a bus service as Halifax at similar size. Boston is like Montréal in that it has a Metro, one of the oldest in the country. Some of its lines are less modern than others, but it does link the entire city. And there is commuter rail service to major suburban communities.

Amtrak, the national passenger rail service does provide good service between Boston and New York City several times per day, also connecting with cities in Connecticut and Rhode Island. The only long distance service does link Boston to Chicago by way of Albany, New York. And Boston is connected through New York City to Washington, D. C. The only service north from Boston extends up to Portland and Brunswick, Maine. And Amtrak does provide passenger rail service between New York City and both Toronto and Montréal, working in conjunction with Via Rail Canada.

Portland and Bar Harbor, Maine do have international ferryboat service connecting them with Nova Scotia and New Brunswick. These ferry boats are capable of transporting cars as well passengers.

There are several small airports throughout the New England states, but only two are significant regional hubs - Boston Logan and Hartford-Springfield. Portland, Maine does have a sizable airport, but it offers few services of any great distance. Boston Logan is a major long distance airport with direct services across the United States, to Canada and overseas primarily to Europe.

THE USE OF THE METRIC SYSTEM: Canada joined the majority of nations of the world by converting to the metric system back in 1973. Among older Canadians, you still hear people speak about feet, miles or pounds, but among the younger generation, metric is now the accepted standard. Thus in Canada, distances are measured in meters and kilometers, liquids are measured in liters and solid weight in kilograms. When watching a weather forecast, temperatures are given in degrees Celsius and wind speed in kilometers while barometric pressure is shown in kilopascals. Yet despite being on the metric system, there is one area in which metric is not used, and there appears to be no rational explanation. When buying real estate or even when renting an apartment, all interior sizes are measured in square feet, yet land is always shown in the metric system by use of hectares. Also if you were to be buying hardwood flooring or carpeting, measurements are given in square feet. This is a rather odd anomaly but one that persists.

When on shore in Canada, you will see only the metric system and Celsius for temperature. There is one easy way to convert Celsius to Fahrenheit in your head without resorting to a calculator. If you see a Celsius temperature on a digital or illuminated sign and you want to convert it to Fahrenheit here is an example as to how to do so without a calculator or pen and paper. Say the Celsius temperature is 10 degrees. Double the number and subtract 10 percent and add 32. The number 10 becomes 20 minus 2 and then you add 32 and you end up with 50 degrees Fahrenheit. Remember the base for Celsius is zero for freezing and 100 for boiling whereas in Fahrenheit the equivalents are 32 and 212 degrees.

The United States persists in remaining off the metric system. Thus on the cruise you will be given weather information in both Celsius and Fahrenheit for temperatures and in kilometers and miles for wind speed. And of course ships navigate under a third maritime system where distances are quoted in nautical miles. One nautical mile is equal to 6,076 feet where a statute mile is equal to 5,280 feet. When the ship's captain makes his noon announcement, he will always give the distance traveled the past day and the current speed in knots, which stands for nautical miles.

THE MEDIA: Canada has an active publishing industry. Canadian authors in both English and French have a wide audience, and bookstores devote much of their shelf space to Canadian literature. The federal government regulates the magazine publishing industry in that foreign publishers that wish to produce a Canadian edition must devote 50 percent of the content to Canadian topics as well as featuring Canadian advertising. This has limited the expansion of American publications into Canada for the sake of adding to their advertising revenue by issuing so called Canadian editions that were nothing more than the American content with Canadian advertising. Newspapers are found in all parts of the country, either in English or French, but the most widely read newspaper is the "Globe and Mail," published in several regional editions.

Radio and television show a distinct competitive trend in that the federal government and private broadcasters vie with each other for market share. The Canadian Broadcasting Corporation, better known as the CBC is a Crown Corporation, heavily funded by the federal government. It produces outstanding programming and also is known for its Monday night hockey and its superb evening news program, "The National." The Canadian Television Network or CTV is second in scope to the CBC. There are numerous local and cable stations now offering greater variety. Throughout the country, English and French radio and television will be found, but in Québec, French stations totally outnumber those broadcasting in English. All radio and television network stations are identified by call letters that begin with "C."

In New England you will find regional magazines, especially ones oriented toward outdoor activities and tourism. Almost every significant community produces a local newspaper, but the most widely read throughout the region are the daily newspapers published in Boston along with USA Today. Radio and television are similar to what you will find in any region of the United States. There are the major networks broadcasting through their local affiliates and then there are the major cable companies. On cable TV the popular news channels are CNN, Fox and MSNBC, but these do not offer regional content.

THE ROLE OF GOVERNMENT IN EACH COUNTRY

Now for a real eye opener! How do the Canadian and American systems of government differ? A simple answer is to say they are like day and night from one another. Canada is a constitutional monarchy with a parliamentary system of public government. The United States is a republic with a separate executive and legislative branch each elected by the public.

I would strongly urge you to go to *www.cbc.ca* on any weeknight at 9 PM Eastern Standard Time and then click on watch and find the screen for *The National*. Or you can go to www.ctvnews.ca at 11 PM Eastern Standard Time. These are the nightly national and world news broadcasts. If you watch one or both, you will immediately see how different Canada is from the United States on many fronts, especially with regard to its government and its worldview. Try it. If you stay in a Canadian hotel either at the start or end of your cruise, I highly recommend watching either CBC *The National* or CTV *News* in the evening just to see how different the two countries are with regard to the news stories you will view, especially those regarding the day-to-day aspects of government. You will be amazed at how different the two countries are. If you are a foreign national, it will still be of interest for you to then watch the American news on television when you are in Boston or New York City.

THE CANADIAN SYSTEM: The Head of State in Canada is His Majesty, Charles III, King of Canada. Yes the British monarch is also the king of 15 Commonwealth countries in addition to the United Kingdom by the choice of each nation. Since he cannot live in Canada or the other 14 Commonwealth nations as well as the United Kingdom, each country's government chooses a Governor General for a specific term of office. He/she becomes the embodiment of the Crown and is the de facto head of state.

Canada's current Governor General is The Right Honourable Mary Simon. She was nominated by the Cabinet and serves for five years as the king's representative. And she is invested with the powers of the Crown. She can dismiss Parliament in the event of any deadlock or scandal. She has the veto power over the Parliament and she is also the head of the armed forces. And it is the Governor General who officially welcomes other heads of state to Canada. But these broad powers are rarely used in Canada or any of the other Commonwealth countries. The last time the British sovereign used the veto power was in the early 1700's. And in the last few decades on the Australian Governor General used the veto power during a national political crisis.

His Majesty, Charles III, King of Canada

Her Excellency Mary Simon, Governor General of Canada

Like the United States government, the Canadian Parliament consists of two houses but that is where the similarities stop:

* **The Senate.** This is called the Upper House. Its 105 members are appointed by the Prime Minister and Cabinet in the lower house and serve to age 75. The seats are apportioned by the population of the provinces. Senators advise the Governor General regarding bills coming up from the lower house as to passage or veto. Only in specific instances can the Senate initiate legislation.

* **The House of Commons** is technically the lower house with 338 elected members, apportioned by the population of the provinces. And herein lies the real power. Members represent a Riding (electoral district). After a federal election, the party that garners the greatest number of seats is charged with forming the Government. The party leader becomes Prime Minister and he/she appoints other important members as Cabinet Ministers to head up the various government departments. Only the party in power normally can introduce legislation.

The Right Honourable Justin Trudeau, Prime Minister of Canada
(Work of Jeangagnon, CC BY SA 4.0, Wikimedia.org)

The leader of the party with the second highest number of seats leads Her Majesty's Loyal Opposition and it is their job to question the Government and hold its feet to the fire so to speak, keeping them honest. If no party wins a majority (169 seats), the party with the highest total forms what is called a minority government, which can be brought down more easily by a vote of no confidence from the opposition. Then a new election would have to be called. If there are no votes of confidence lost, the Government does not need to call another election for four years. The next election for the House of Commons will occur in October 2023. At the moment the Liberal Party, which is in power, has been rocked by a scandal that caused a loss of majority status. Of the three major national parties, government has to date always been formed by either the Liberal or Conservative Parties. But the New Democratic Party, the Bloc Québécois and the Green Party all hold significant seats in the House of Commons.

Canadian House of Commons, (Work of Jeangagnon, CC BY SA 4.0, Wikimedia.org)

Provincial governments function along lines similar to the federal parliament, but not all provincial parliaments have two houses. The head of state in each province is the Lieutenant Governor representing the Crown. The parliamentary leader in a province is known as the Premier. Not all of the provinces have a bicameral legislature with an upper and lower house.

When federal or provincial elections are held, the campaign period is short, generally under three months. Unless an election has been the result of a vote of no confidence, the set date is the second Tuesday of October every fourth year, a process that began in 2007. Prior to that change in policy, the maximum period had been five years between elections.

Canada has a Supreme Court, its members appointed by the Cabinet. But three members must always be from the province of Québec. The provincial and lower courts in each province are appointed by their parliaments, but all work under one national code of justice.

Canada has as an advisory body to the Government that is known as the Privy Council made up of the Governor General, Prime Minister, Leader of the Opposition and the President of the Senate and prominent citizens who hold the Order of Canada, a prestigious honor. They hold a traditional degree of nominal power by force of their advice. This is a carryover of a tradition from the United Kingdom.

THE AMERICAN SYSTEM: The way in which government operates in the United States is very different from Canada. It is a more rigid system with no flexibility on when elections are held. Opposing parties can also have control of the Executive and Legislative Branches at the same time.

The President is the head of state, elected along with a Vice President, in a national election held once every four years on the first Tuesday after the first Monday in November. The term of office is four years with one renewal for a maximum of eight years.

The Honorable Joseph Biden, President of the United States

There is both a popular vote, but a rather archaic carry over from the early years when the public was not well informed has the ultimate power. This is the Electoral College, given so many votes per state based upon population. The Electoral College is expected to award the whole number of votes per state to the popular vote leader. In 2000, George W. Bush won the Electoral College vote, but Al Gore had over 500,000 more popular votes but lost. And in 2016, Donald Trump won the Electoral College vote, but Hillary Clinton had over 3,000,000 more popular votes but also lost. In the 2020 election, Joseph Biden won a 6,000,000 popular majority and by distribution it translated to over 300 Electoral College votes.

The Congress of the United States is divided into an upper and lower house each with its own distinct powers:

* **The Senate** is the upper house with two senators from each state regardless of population. The 100 members have many exclusive legislative functions such as the approval of foreign treaties and the confirmation of high-ranking government appointments. Senators serve for six years with 1/3 elected at each two-year federal election. The Vice President of the United States presides over the Senate, but each party has a Senate leader who wields a lot of power, especially the leader of the majority party.

The U. S. Senate Chamber

* **The House of Representatives** has 435 voting members representing the states by population and two non-voting members. Members are up for election every two years. The House has a wide range of responsibilities first and foremost is physical expenditures being the keeper of the federal purse. The

Speaker of the House is elected from among the membership of the party with the highest number of seats. The leader of the majority power is also a very influential member. The Speaker of the House is the third most powerful leader after the President and Vice President.

On most pieces of legislation there must be concurrence and compromise between the Senate and House of Representatives. Unlike the Canadian Parliament, this means that a lot of time can be wasted in exacting compromise if the two houses are ruled over by opposing political parties.

The President of the United States has the ultimate veto power, but can be overruled if the Congress is led by the opposing major political party and they have sufficient votes. But such a scenario is somewhat rare.

The Supreme Court of the United States has nine justices, appointed by the President of the United States when vacancies arise, but with majority approval from the Senate. Members may serve for life, but often step down past age 70. State courts are independent of the Supreme Court, but can be overruled if a case is brought to the highest court of the land. There are federal crimes and United States district courts to handle their disposition, but most cases are heard in state run courts. Many judges at lower and mid-levels are elected by the public at large, a great difference from the Canadian system where all judges are appointed and serve the Crown.

Each state has a similar legislature, though it need not have two houses. And the separately elected head of the state is the Governor.

COMPARISON AND CONTRAST: As you can see, one of the greatest areas of difference between Canada and the United States comes in the area of government with Canada being a constitutional monarchy and the United States being a republic. Citizens of each country are very proud of their system of government, and I as a dual citizen see the merits and pitfalls of each.

The governments of the two countries work closely together on many issues, especially economic relations. Each is the other's leading trade partner and thus the economies of Canada and the United States are heavily intertwined. When it comes to how each country functions globally, they are the closest of allies but do not always agree as to issues or how to proceed. In late 2015, Canada announced that it would pull its fighter jets out of the coalition bombing of ISIS targets in Syria. Canada contributed jets to the bombing mission under the former Conservative government of Prime Minister Stephen Harper. Liberal Prime Minister Justin Trudeau felt Canada could best serve the coalition in other ways, not through continued bombing runs. President Barak Obama had expressed disappointment at this decision. Until recently the most strained period of relations came during the administration of Prime Minister Pierre Trudeau when Canada would not condone United States military action in Vietnam and when it extended diplomatic relations to the People's Republic of China.

Since 2017 President Donald Trump and Prime Minister Justin Trudeau did not seen eye to eye over the future of the North American Free Trade Agreement. Also both leaders held opposing views on environmental protection with Canada aiming toward becoming as green a nation as possible in the near future. All through the Trump administration, Canada and the United States had what could be called edgy relations essentially because President Trump was convinced that economically Canada was taking advantage of the United States on many issues. Relations should vastly improve under the new Biden administration.

There is greater overall flexibility in the Canadian political system. The government is not locked into absolutely fixed terms of office, and is more attuned to the wishes of the populace. But of course with a population one tenth that of the United States it is possible for there to be closer ties between the government and the public. Canadians take a much greater interest in their national and provincial politics. The percentage of eligible voters that actually cast a ballot is normally higher than in the United States.

THE FORMAT FOR PORTS OF CALL CHAPTERS

To present you with the most comprehensive, yet personalized view of each of the ports of call in eastern Canada and New England, I have established a set pattern for the writing of each chapter. In this way, you will have a consistency with regard to finding needed information when searching for any aspect of a particular port.

Each chapter is organized in the following manner:

* The where factor - With maps and text, the location of each port of call is presented with regard to both its physical location and its geopolitical position within a Canadian province of American state.

* The natural setting - It is important to have an idea as to the geographic setting of the port, be it on a bay, river estuary or inland along a major river. You will be able to have a better understanding of the landscape and topography of each port of call and its surroundings. This will help you to visualize each port you are to be visiting.

* A brief local history - Once again you may feel that the historic aspect is being overly emphasized. But keep in mind that to fully understand a port of call you must know how it came into being, what its historic role has been and what important buildings and monuments add to the overall ambiance of the community. You can visually see history all around you, but to understand it there must be some historic context, which this section provides.

* The physical layout of the port of call - Again using maps and text along with numerous photographs, you will be presented with a geographic picture of the port of call.

* The major venues that are important to visit - This will present you with all of the significant places of interest, including historic sites, museums, forts, battlefields and government buildings that are the backbone of the community. Also points of interest that are considered to be purely "fun" locations are also presented.

* Suggested tours - This important section will give you suggestions as to how to get around either by tours offered through the cruise line, local hop-on-hop-

off bus, private guide with car, rental car or on foot. Each mode of transport will be evaluated with pros and cons.

* Places to dine - I limit the places to dine to those serving local cuisine primarily for lunch since on a cruise you are generally back out at sea during dinner time. I believe it is important to sample local cuisine to fully appreciate the lifestyle of each port of call.

* Places to shop – As for shopping, I also attempt to present those shops that sell local handcrafts and good quality gift items. But I on occasion will note major department stores if I consider them to be significant such as in Montréal.

Unlike the major tour books, I am presenting only the best of local sights and eating establishments because your time is limited. Too much overload of information will in the end bog you down with making decisions as to where to go, what to do and where to eat. On average you only have between six and ten hours in a port of call, so I have designed my chapters to help you maximize your time on shore.

I do present hotel information for Montréal, New York and Boston since these are three ports of call where tours begin or terminate. New York is so large and famous and that there are dozens of reference books on such a major city, I have only provided a listing of what I consider the absolute best hotels in both the four and five-star categories along with a few select places to dine. My choices are based upon my long years of experience traveling in Atlantic Canada and New England.

MAJOR NEW ENGLAND PORTS OF CALL

Map of New England shores, (© OpenStreetMap contributors)

The eastern Canada and New England fall cruises definitely place more emphasis upon Canadian ports because the region is larger and far more diverse than its American counterpart. Among the potential ports of call within the U. S., the only two that can be considered as major are Portland, Maine and Boston, Massachusetts. With the majority of such cruises either beginning or terminating in New York City, it is also included in this volume, but it is of course not in New England. These chapters will provide information on the important ports of call, giving recommendations as to sightseeing, shopping and dining after first introducing you to their respective states and providing some essential geographic and historic information. Once again the aim is to provide you with the necessary tools so that when you arrive, you have the background needed to fully appreciate where you are visiting. There are also choice hotel recommendations for Boston because many shorter cruises begin or terminate here. And there are also a few choice hotel recommendations for New York City.

There are four minor ports that vary with tour itineraries, but these follow in separate chapters in this volume after the major ports of call. The first two chapters concentrate on Portland and Boston, two cities that each offers much to see. Some cruises will either begin or terminate in Boston, but the vast majority of cruise itineraries use New York in the third chapter on major ports of call, as it is the port of embarkation or termination for the vast majority of these cruises.

For those of you who are American residents, you will find that New England cities offer all the conveniences and brand names that you are accustomed to all over the country. But unlike the rest of the nation, New England is geographically quite distinct. It is the most unique cultural region within the country. The typical New England wood house, often whitewashed and with window shutters is much more widely used than one would expect. And the white town church with its tall steeple, which has been immortalized in Christmas cards for decades, is very real and found throughout New England in its smaller towns and cities. In the major cities brick townhouses tend to dominate, their narrow fronts facing the street with small porches. Churches are also constructed of brick, but their tapering white spires also pierce the sky in a similar manner as the country towns.

Wood houses and picket fences so typify New England, as seen here in Newport, Rhode Island

Many New England traditions include clam bakes on the beach, strong patriotism and flying of the flag, close family and church ties, a love of gardening and the out of doors. These are but a few of the characteristics of this region. And then there is the pattern of speech, the so called "Yankee" or New England accent. It varies from one state to the next, but once you are out on the street of your first port, you will know you are in New England.

Boston is the largest and grandest city in New England with a metropolitan population of several million. Thus not everyone is a native New Englander. The city is very much a melting pot, but during the 19th century it did see a large number of both Irish and Italian immigrants. Portland is not a major industrial city and thus its roots are more traditional of what you expect to see in New England. Visiting the two major ports will give you a stronger understanding of this region.

If you are not an American resident, the New England region will appear to have a very strong degree of charm, which you will should fully appreciate for its deep roots as being one of the first major regions settled during Colonial times. You will see many traits and even architectural features that are more akin to the British Isles or even Canada. Many Canadian visitors often feel that New England reminds them more of the Atlantic Provinces. And this is a valid observation since both share many elements of Colonial history. Australian visitors also find that they feel quite comfortable in New England, as it reminds them to a degree of many of their smaller country towns in the eastern part of Australia.

No matter where you are from, you will find that the two major port of call will be of great interest because of their Colonial roots as seen in the architecture and in many daily elements of the culture. And if your itinerary includes any of the lesser ports, this interest will only grow even stronger.

PORTLAND, MAINE

Map of greater Portland, Maine, (© OpenStreetMap contributors)

If your ship left Montréal, your first American port of call will either be Bar Harbor or Portland. Bar Harbor is one of the less frequently visited ports and will be treated in a later chapter. But the majority of southbound itineraries will have Portland, Maine as the first port of call after leaving either Halifax or St. John. And it will be in Portland that your ship will clear United States immigration and customs. On smaller ships the immigration formalities are normally handled onboard ship. For the majority of northbound cruises Portland will be your last American port of call before entering Canada.

THE NATURAL SETTING OF THE STATE OF MAINE: Of the six New England states, Maine is the most northeasterly, the only mainland state in the United States that shares a border with just one other state, which is New Hampshire. The rest of its land border is with Canada. With 91,646 square kilometers or 35,385 square miles Maine is the largest of the New England States, actually larger in physical size than the other five states combined. Maine is thought of as being the most easterly state in the United States while

Alaska is clearly the most westerly. But in reality, Alaska is also the most easterly state. Now how can this be? If you look at a globe or a world map, you will find that the Aleutian Islands of Alaska extend so far west that they cross the 180 degree line of longitude and the farthest islands are in reality in the Eastern Hemisphere. However, the International Dateline has been adjusted around these islands to keep their calendar the same as the rest of the nation. This also holds true for the farthest eastern tip of Siberia, which means that Russia extends so far east that it stretches into a tiny bit of the Western Hemisphere. And again the International Dateline has been adjusted. So next time someone asks a trivia question that reads, "What is the most easterly state in the United States?" The answer is NOT Maine. It is Alaska!

Yet Maine only has 1,330,000 residents, the majority living in the near coastal region, primarily in urban communities. On a per square kilometer or mile basis, Maine is the least populated state in the United States east of the Mississippi River. This leaves most of the state's interior virtually empty, making it the only New England state that essentially contains vast wilderness regions where bears, moose and deer roam unhindered. However, there are several private tracts of land belonging to major lumber companies and the public is rarely given access. This is a state where outdoor pursuits such as hunting, fishing, hiking and kayaking are still practiced on a large scale. When it comes to the out of doors, the most famous national apparel company that specializes in outdoor clothing is located in Maine. And I am speaking of none other than L. L. Bean.

Most of northern Maine falls within the Appalachian Mountain chain. Here long parallel ranges and intervening valleys dominate the landscape. The mountains are heavily forested, and for this reason Maine is known as "The Pine Tree State." The southern half of main contains a variety of lower mountain ranges, and the forests are more temperate, showing a mix of broadleaf, deciduous trees along with pine. But the entire state was heavily glaciated, thus softer sediments were scoured away leaving behind a base of hard, more resistant rock. And through glacial action, the state is pockmarked with hundreds of lakes that vary in size from small ponds to some of the larges lakes in the region.

The Maine coastline is very irregular and contains dozens of sheltered bays, small coves and offshore islands. As glacial ice eroded the coastline, it detached many hard rock pieces, creating islands when sea level again rose. This gives the coastline intense beauty and is one of the state's great selling points for tourism.

Climatically the near coastal areas are more temperate, having cool summers and often plagued by fog. Winters are cold, but will see a mix of rain and snow in most years. But inland, away from the sea, a cold winter continental climatic pattern emerges. The deep interior of Maine has brutally cold and very snowy winters.

The Portland Head Lighthouse is an icon among lighthouses

HISTORY OF MAINE SETTLEMENT:
Of all the states in the nation, Maine is definitely known to have seen Viking explorers at the start of the 13th century, trading with the Penobscot tribe, one of the Algonquin peoples of the region. The Vikings had occupied Iceland and Greenland in the 11th century, and they attempted settlement in Newfoundland but were not successful. Yet they still had an interest in trade, especially for timber since within the first few centuries of occupancy in Iceland they had exhausted their wood supply.

The French did establish settlement on Saint Croix Island in 1604, the famous French explorer of eastern Canada, Samuel de Champlain, being one of the founders. This is the start of a larger region known as Acadia. They later did establish Jesuit missions in Penobscot Bay and on Mount Desert Island along with the creation of Fort Pentagouet to protect a third settlement called Castine. But ultimately the French saw New Brunswick and Nova Scotia as more productive.

The British attempted settlement in 1607, 14 years before the Mayflower reached the Massachusetts shores. But the settlement of Popham failed after just over a year and the colonists returned to England. A second British colonial settlement was made in 1623, but again that settlement also failed.

Maine was never given colonial status, but rather it became part of the Massachusetts Bay Colony in 1652. When the British seriously started to settle Maine in the 1680's, there were skirmishes with the native peoples who were ultimately killed or driven out by British soldiers. And there were also numerous military engagements with French forces since the French had considered Maine to be part of Acadia even though they did not truly settle the territory.

Skirmishes with native tribes and the French continued until the British defeated both in Nova Scotia. At that time, the eastern part of Maine, along with New Brunswick were considered a part of the Colony of Nova Scotia. Western Maine was part of Massachusetts, however, a 13-mile coastal strip of New Hampshire interrupted the two territories.

When the American Revolutionary War was concluded with victory for the new nation, the treaty that ended the conflict did not clarify the border with between Maine and New Brunswick. The final border treaty was concluded in 1842, two decades after Maine had become a separate state. Maine became a state in 1820 after prior denial of its wish to secede from Massachusetts. The entry of Maine to the Union was concurrent with the entry of Missouri, this being a compromise where Maine was admitted as a free state and Missouri as a slave holding state.

Originally Portland was the state capital, as it was the largest city. But the capital was moved in 1832 to Augusta because of its more central location. The state remained somewhat of a cultural backwater, considered to be an outlier to the rest of New England until the early 20th century when wealthy Bostonians and New Yorkers discovered its southern coast. Into the 20th century, Maine has been recognized for its hunting and fishing, raising of potatoes and its southern coastal beach resorts such as Kennebunkport. To this day, Maine remains somewhat remote in the minds of most Americans. But the residents seem to not take any offense, and they love the fact that their state is somewhat isolated from the rest of the nation.

A LOCAL HISTORY OF PORTLAND: The initial settlement of Portland began in 1623 under the name of Casco Bay, but this colony was unsuccessful. In 1643, a new settlement based more upon fishing and trade was established, and it was simply called Casco. It was absorbed into the Massachusetts Bay Colony in 1658 and the name was changed to Falmouth. The town slowly grew and took root, but in 1676 it was destroyed by the local Abenaki tribe as part of a protracted war between the natives and the colonists. It was rebuilt only to be destroyed again in 1690 by a combined French and native raiding party. During the American Revolutionary War, Falmouth was burned once again in 1775, this time rebuilt and the name changed to Portland. Given its good anchorage and access to the interior, it was natural for Portland to become a major port, though it has seen its ups and downs during the early years after the revolution because of the Embargo Act of 1807, which prohibited trade with Britain.

When Portland lost the capital to Augusta in 1832, many residents though this would doom the community to a second-class status. But its importance as a trade center turned out to be far more important than its role as the capital. And through the decades, its role as the financial and commercial hub of the state has continued to growth. The selection of Portland to be the ice free port for Montréal and the building of the Grand Trunk Railroad line in 1853 from Canada assured the continued success of the port. However, ultimately the Canadian National Railroad completed a line to St. John, New Brunswick keeping goods totally within Canada, but that was not until 1923. During the period from 1853 to 1923, Portland became a major railroad hub for northern New England and also the site for the manufacture of railroad steam engines.

During the American Civil War, a Confederate raiding party tried to take Portland and a small naval battle ensued. This became the northernmost battle of the Civil War. At the end of the war, during the 1866 Independence Day festivities, a fireworks display got out of control and burned much of the city's downtown core. After that event, most of the rebuilding was done in brick.

As Portland grew and suburban development spread away from the central peninsula, the downtown area began to show signs of neglect. But the city invested heavily in the infrastructure to revitalize Old Portland, especially with the coming of the cruise ship traffic. Today downtown Portland is quite an active commercial zone and it merges with the Old Portland waterfront. Many fashionable apartment and condominium blocks have developed downtown, with some moderate high-rise construction in the architectural mix. And the waterfront has become a popular location for seafood restaurants, most specializing in Maine lobster and other seafood dishes.

CRUISE SHIP TERMINAL: Cruise ships dock at a large terminal facility immediately to the east of the principal Old Town waterfront with its many boutiques and restaurants. It is very convenient for those who do not go on tours and just wish to walk in the heart of the city.

For southbound cruises that do not visit Bar Harbor, Portland becomes the port of entry. Immigration is held either on board ship or in the terminal facility before passengers may disembark. Tour busses, privately secured tour vehicles and taxis all wait at the street side end of the terminal.

THE PHYSICAL LAYOUT OF PORTLAND: Most cruise ships spend a full day in Portland, some even staying until the late evening hours. The cruise terminal is located immediately adjacent to the downtown area, making it very convenient for passengers to walk to all the major historic venues and many of the outstanding eateries along the waterfront. Longer tours are offered to visit Kennebunkport and to Freeport, home to L. L. Bean and many outlet shops.

Portland is the largest city in Maine, its population stands at 204,000 with nearly 500,000 in its immediate trade area. Thus just over one third of Maine's population is within the greater Portland area.

The Portland skyline seen from the deck of an arriving ship

Suburban Portland is heavily wooded and beautiful

The city surrounds the estuary of the Fore River where it creates a large bay filled with sizeable rocky islands, some of them containing homes. The heart of the city occupies a rather hilly peninsula that is bounded on the south by the Fore River, and on the north by Back Cove, a smaller enclave of the greater estuary. The entire region once had a thick forest of broadleaf deciduous trees mixed with some pine, but today much of the land is either urbanized or devoted to farming, with many woodlots containing the remainders of the forest.

The outer islands break the incoming waves, leaving the actual harbor very calm, and it was this protected anchorage combined with a source of fresh water that was conducive to settlement. Many of the outer islands in the bay are inhabited and connected to downtown by small ferryboats.

As an old colonial city, Portland does not have a very regular street pattern, however, on the main peninsula the streets do tend to intersect for the most part at right angles. Beyond the peninsula, suburban Portland tends to fan outward on both sides of the bay in an irregular manner, as seen on the maps at the end of the chapter. But being a small city with little major traffic, it is not difficult for visitors with a rental car to find their way around the city.

The colonial flavor of downtown Portland

The climate is classed as continental, but there is a definite maritime influence, especially during summer, as days are cool and fogs are frequent. In winter, there is a mix of cold, blustery days with rain or snow. Some years the city is actually blanketed by heavy snow.

WHAT TO SEE AND DO: Most cruise ships will spend a full day in Portland, but when coming south, this becomes the port of entry into the United States. Immigration officials normally like to conduct a face-to-face immigration inspection, which can take an hour or more of time before passengers leave the ship. Some cruise lines will arrive at Noon or 1 PM on their southbound itineraries, leaving only a few hours of daylight, but they do stay until 9 or 10 PM. This does allow for an evening out to dinner since the majority of guests would like to sample Maine lobster. Fortunately there are numerous seafood restaurants along the waterfront just a short walk from the cruise ship dock.

Here are the options available to you for touring in and around Portland:

* **Ship sponsored tours** – Most cruise lines offer a four-hour introductory tour of the main city highlights either by motor coach or on foot or a

combination of both tours. And depending upon the cruise line, some offer tours to Kennebunkport or shopping tours to L. L. Bean, and still others offer harbour and island cruises on small pleasure craft.

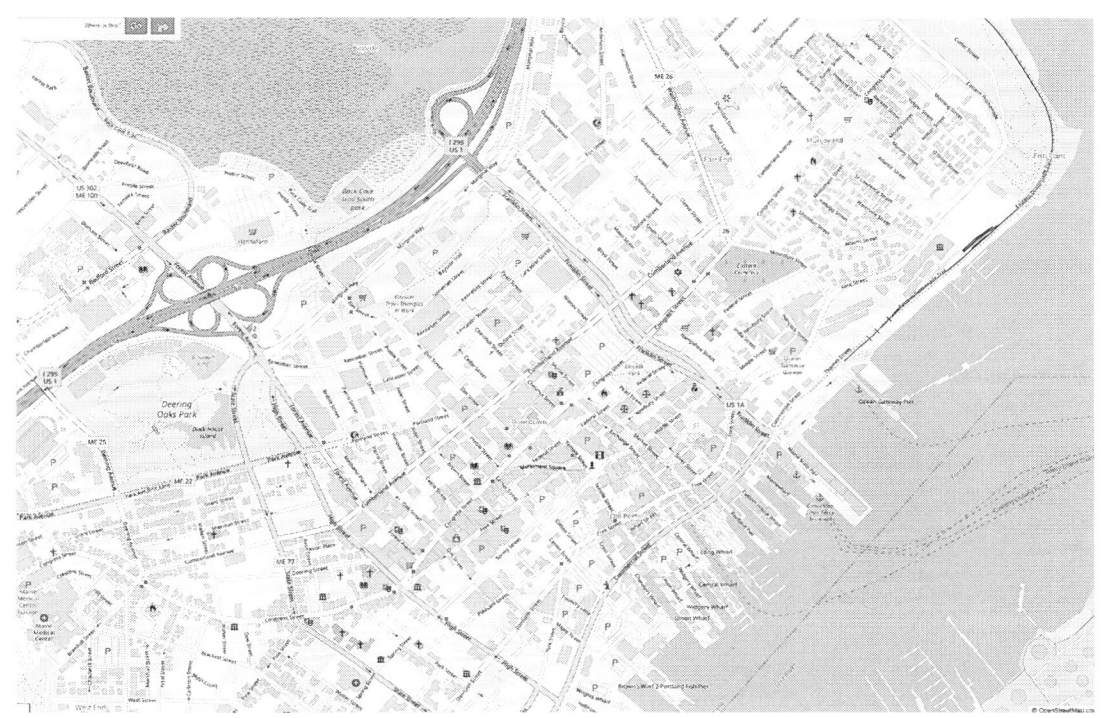

Map of downtown Portland, (© OpenStreetMap contributors)

* **Private car and driver** – A private car and driver/guide is only needed if you want to take a personalized tour around the entire city or out into the surrounding countryside. There are often ship sponsored tours to Kennebunkport and Freeport, or you could arrange a private tour through the shore excursion desk or through Maine Day Trip Tours at www.mainedaytrip.com . Another provider of private tours is Tours by Locals. Check out their web offerings at www.toursbylocals.com/Portland-Maine-Tours .

** **There is a hop on hop of trolley** that enables you to tour all the major highlights of the city at your own pace. For detailed information visit their web page at www.graylineofportland.com/Information .

* **Taxi tours** – A few taxis will be found at the gate to the cruise terminal and they can provide local or out of town tours on an hourly basis upon request.

* **Water taxi tours** – www.portlandharborwatertours.com for details on their various offerings.

* **Walking** on your own – If you simply want to tour around the city center and Old Portland, you can easily do so on foot. The downtown core is relatively large, but quite fascinating and you will get some good exercise.

MAJOR SIGHTS: Portland has a definite charm and flavor that speaks primarily to the 19th century with a heavy dose of the Victorian Era. The Old Town and downtown offer prime examples of approximately two hundred plus years of growth. My recommendation on the major sights that are must see within Portland, shown alphabetically,
 are:

* **Commercial Street** - Walk this main waterfront promenade and the side streets leading off of it to get the flavor of Old Portland. You will also find some of the best seafood restaurants in the city along this street along with many boutiques and shops catering to visitors. And there are many coffee shops and restaurants on this waterfront street

Congress Street is the heart of modern downtown Portland

* **Congress Street** – This is the main shopping and financial street for the city of Portland. Most of the buildings, including the few high rise office blocks, date back to the 1930's and 40's and blend with the Old Town area adjacent to the downtown core.

* **Harbor Fish Market** – On the waterfront at 9 Custom House Wharf, you will see the vast array of fresh fish and seafood that is caught in local waters. Residents and restaurant chefs come early to get the best of the daily catch. The market is open Monday thru Saturday from 8:30 AM to 6 PM and from 9 AM to 4 PM on Sunday.

* **Maine Narrow Gauge Railroad and Museum** - Located right outside the cruise terminal and a bit to the left, the railway museum will be well received by anyone who loves trains. And they have a narrow gauge train that makes a circle of the main city peninsula every hour starting at 10 AM through the middle of October. The last one-hour train ride leaves the depot at 3 PM. Visit their web page at www.mainenarrowgauge.org for details.

The historic Portland City Hall

* **Portland City Hall** – The city hall building is a rather grand building at 389 Congress Street. Built in 1909 this building is constructed of granite and is especially imposing given the small size of the city. It is open weekdays between 8:30 AM and 4:30 PM but no specific tours are given.

* **Portland Head Light** - This old lighthouse is now the most famous and visited in Maine. It occupies the outer edge of the harbor entrance and can be seen from the ship. But a visit is a very special event, but can only be done as part of an organized tour. It is Maine's oldest lighthouse built in 1791. Visits to the park surrounding the lighthouse are permitted from sunrise to sunset. You may also get good pictures of the lighthouse from the port side of your ship when it sails into the Portland Harbor providing it is not foggy. The United States Coast Guard is still responsible for the operation of the lighthouse, but the park surrounding it is run by the suburban community of Cape Elizabeth. The museum is open daily from 10 AM to 4 PM but the actual lighthouse is not open to the public.

* **Portland Museum of Art** - For a small city, Portland has an outstanding art museum containing a fine collection of New England artists in both landscape and portraiture. The museum is the pride of the city. Located at 7 Congress Square, it is within walking distance of the cruise terminal. Open 10 AM to 5 PM daily.

The skyline of downtown Portland from the Observatory

* **Portland Observatory** - This tall wood structure sits atop the highest hill on the main city peninsula and on a clear day it affords a fantastic view of the city and its surroundings. It was built in the early 1800's and its construction alone is worthy of a visit. It is located at 138 Congress Street, a good walk from the ship up some steep hills. The observatory is open from 10 AM to 4:30 PM, but only into the middle of October.

Old Town Portland – Along the waterfront and extending inland to Congress Street is where you find the oldest buildings dating back into the Colonial Era and the 18th century. This part of Portland is a small version of Boston with its colonial charm.

Second Street in historic Old Town Portland

* **Victoria Mansion** – At 109 Danforth Street, this former mansion is now a museum and its artifacts and furnishings are a testament to the elegance of the Victorian Era in Portland among the elite of the city. The museum is open through the end of October from 10 AM to 3:45 PM daily.

* **Wadsworth-Longfellow House and Gardens** - The home of the famous American poet Henry Wadsworth-Longfellow is not a museum that chronicles the life of this major literary figure. It is located at 489 Congress Street, a bit of a walk from the ship, but it can be reached via the hop on hop off trolley or

taxi. The museum is open from 10 AM to 4 PM Tuesday thru Saturday until the end of October.

The home of the great poet Wadsworth-Longfellow

SIGHTS OUTSIDE OF THE CITY: Outside of Portland I offer two places that are worth visiting if you want to travel out of the city, Some cruise lines may offer a tour to either location, but if your ship does not, you can easily find a taxi along the waterfront outside of the cruise pier that will provide service at an hourly rate.

* **Freeport** - Located 28 kilometers or 17 miles north of Portland, this small colonial town is noted more for shopping than anything else. It is home to a large number of brand name outlet stores, and it is the headquarters for L. L. Bean, presenting the flagship store that many cannot wait to visit. Some cruise itineraries do offer a shopping tour to L. L. Bean, otherwise you will need to have a rental car or car and driver.

* **Kennebunkport** - Located 48 kilometers or 30 miles south of Portland, this old fishing and whaling port became a popular getaway for wealthy city dwellers from Boston and New York. It offers beautiful beaches, a mix of architectural styles and the homes of the rich and famous, including the family compound of the Bush Family. There is also a wonderful trolley museum in

Kennebunkport. Many cruise itineraries offer a full or half-day tour to Kennebunkport, which is your best option, as the structure of the tour will show you all the highlights often from both a land and water perspective. Arranging for a car and driver/guide is a more expensive, but more personalized option. Opting to rent a car and drive on your own is less expensive, but you will not see as many of the important sights.

Fall crowds in Kennebunkport< (Work of Captain-tucker, CC BY SA 3.0, Wikimedia.org)

DINING OUT: You absolutely must at least have lunch in Portland, or dinner if your ship is staying late, to sample some of the freshest seafood you will find anywhere. The city is noted for its fishing fleet and the quality of its lobster, haddock, cod, mussels, clams and more. There are so many good restaurants in Portland, and yes some are more diverse in offering meats, poultry and ethnic dishes. I have simply chosen to mention those that are famous for seafood, as this is what most visitors want. There are also numerous craft breweries in the city center that have a great reputation, but unfortunately I am not one to recommend any since I am not a beer lover. My recommendations for restaurants, shown alphabetically, are:

* **Back Bay Grill** – At 65 Portland Street, this is without a doubt one of the top seafood restaurants in all of Maine. But in addition to seafood, they also offer a wide array of meat and poultry dishes, all expertly prepared. And they offer vegetarian dishes as well. They are open Tuesday thru Saturday from 5 to 9 PM and reservations are a must. Call 207 772 8833 to book a table.

* **DiMillo's** on the water at 25 Long Wharf close to the cruise terminal is actually a moored boat converted to a dining room. It is well known and very popular among locals. They can get crowded, but without a reservation during peak lunch or dinner hours you may have a long wait. They are open Noon to 9 PM Monday thru Saturday. Call ahead for reservations at 207 772 2216 otherwise you could have as long as an hour to wait for a table.

* **Emilitsa** – At 547 Congress Street, this is a fine dining establishment with a seafood twist that is Greek and Mediterranean. The flavors are superb along with an congenial atmosphere and good service. They are open Tuesday thru Saturday from 5 to 9 PM. Call them at 207 221 0245 to book a table.

* **Eventide Oyster House** - Located at 85 Middle Street in the city center, they are noted for their fresh seafood, and specialize in oysters. They are a bit pricier than other seafood restaurants, but they do have their loyal following. Hours are from 11 AM to 9 PM daily. Reservations are a must for dinner. Call 207 774 8538 to book a table.

* **Marcy's Diner** - In the city center at 47 Oak Street, this fine restaurant is noted for its variety of homemade soups. They have an extensive menu and do not simply specialize in seafood. Their hours are from 9AM to 2 PM, serving good breakfasts and excellent lunches only Thursday thru Sunday. Reservations are not necessary.

* **Portland Lobster Company** - At 180 Commercial Street, this is a very popular restaurant among visitors. It is crowded, so you might have to wait at prime dining hours. They open at 11 AM and stay open until 10 PM. Call to reserve a table at 207 775 2112.

* **Street and Company** - At 33 Wharf Street, this is a well-known seafood restaurant where Maine lobster is a specialty. It is only open for dinner from 9 to 9 PM daily but extended closing at 10 PM Friday and Saturday and 9:30 PM on Thursday. Reservations are a must. Call 207 775 0887 to book in advance.

SHOPPING: There are numerous shopping venues, especially for local crafts and antiques, which many people come to New England specifically to buy.

* **Commercial Street** - There are numerous small shops along Commercial Street selling a variety of craft and art items.

Shops along Commercial Street

* **Edgecomb Pottery Gallery** - Located at 145 Commercial Street, you will find a great variety of locally made artistic pottery pieces in all sizes and price ranges.

* **L. L. Bean** - In Freeport, it is better than shopping on line or from their catalogue. This is the one place where you will find all of their product line available and on display.

FINAL WORDS: Many cruise guests have little idea as to what they may expect to find in Portland, Maine. Most Americans know a bout the much larger city of Portland, Oregon, but this city is not well known, so expectations are generally not that high. But from my experience, I have not heard anyone say that they did not enjoy spending a day in Portland. And during mid to late fall, the city is definitely ablaze with beautiful colors, and the foliage is even better if you get out into the surrounding countryside.

BOSTON, MASSACHUSETTS

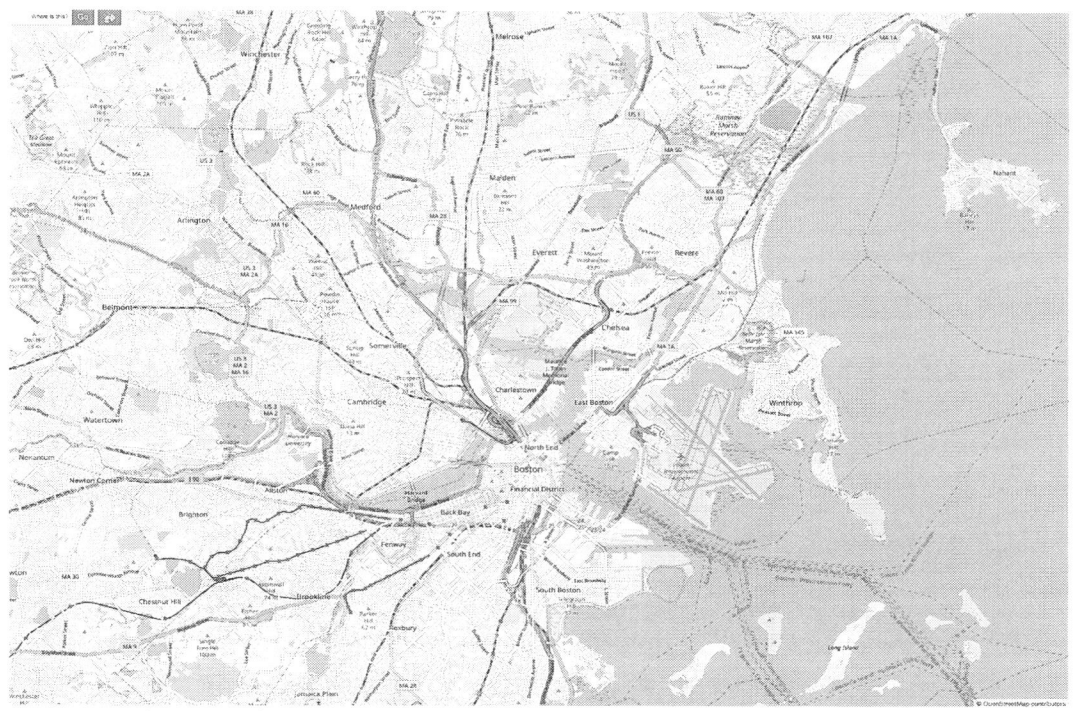

A map of greater Boston, (© OpenStreetMap contributors)

THE NATURAL SETTING OF MASSACHUSETTS: The state of Massachusetts is the seventh smallest state in the U. S. in land area, occupying 27,337 square kilometers or 10,555 square miles. However, it is the most populous state in New England with 6,750,000 residents. What accounts for this high population is the city of Boston and its large suburban ring. Boston is also the largest New England city and based upon its metropolitan area population it is essentially tied with Phoenix, Arizona as the largest capital city region in the country although Phoenix has a greater population within its corporate limits.

Despite its small size, Massachusetts is geographically quite a diverse state, primarily because of its east to west orientation. The far eastern quarter of the state is comprised of low, sandy glacial deposits that include the greater Boston area and Cape Cod, which is a hooked sand spit extending quite a distance out into the Atlantic Ocean and providing for a massive sheltered bay on which the city of Boston is located. Central Massachusetts is a region of low hills with intervening valleys that is dotted with several small lakes and ponds, having been heavily glaciated during the last ice age. This is a beautiful part of the state, still essentially rural and containing many colonial villages. Both the coastal lowlands and the central region are cloaked in mixed woodland of broadleaf deciduous trees that exhibit stunning fall colors.

The Valley of the Connecticut River slices across west central Massachusetts. This valley is typical of a mature river with extensive bottomlands and elevated bluffs on its flanks. The river valley is home to a mix of urban and agricultural pursuits. Springfield, the state's second major urban center, is located here.

Western Massachusetts is part of the Appalachian Mountain chain, known locally as the Berkshire Mountains. These mountains are gently folded and present ridges and valleys that are oriented north to south. The forests of the Berkshires are essentially mixed between pine and broadleaf deciduous, and again are exceptionally striking during the fall. This is the most popular weekend getaway location for Boston residents and also people from the heavily populated state of Connecticut to the south. The landscape of the Berkshires is similar to that of Vermont, but being closer to large urban centers, it is very well developed.

The beauty of the interior of Massachusetts, (Work of Coolkayaker1, CC BY SA 4.0, Wikimedia.org)

The climates of Massachusetts grow more severe as you move from the coast to the western border. Summer throughout the state is mild, but the coastal lowlands can sometimes be quite warm and humid or at other times damp and foggy. The central and western parts of the state are cooler, especially where elevation factors in. The highest of the Berkshires are over 1,000 meters or 3,000 feet, and here summer temperatures can be about 8 degrees Celsius or 15 degrees Fahrenheit cooler than Boston.

In winter the entire state experiences blustery cold weather, more intense the farther inland from the sea. In 2015, Boston had its snowiest winter on record, as did much of the state, literally burying the cities for weeks at a time. But in some years, the coastal regions receive a mix of rain, sleet and snow.

Summer homes with that typical New England style crowd Cape Cod

A BRIEF MASSACHUSETTS HISTORY: Of all the American states, the history of Massachusetts and Virginia is the most complex since these are the two oldest colonial states. This historic synopsis will be brief because there are hundreds of texts about Colonial America that provide detailed accounts of events in Massachusetts. But a bit of detail here will help you in appreciating just how significant the city of Boston is in America's development.

Boston was one of the two great Colonial cities, and it was also a hotbed of revolution, thus it figured so prominently in the American Revolutionary War.

And when you visit Boston so much of what you will be seeing relates back to its Colonial history and the American Revolution. It is really not possible for any visitor, American or foreign, to appreciate the city of Boston with all of its monuments and public venues without comprehending the city's colonial history and role in the Revolutionary War. This is also true of the city of Philadelphia, but it does not go back as far as Boston in pre-revolutionary times.

Every year when Americans celebrate Thanksgiving, they are paying homage to the Pilgrims, a group of religious dissidents who came over on the Mayflower in 1620 and started the Plymouth Colony, the location of which is a short distance south of present day downtown Boston. Their survival was tenuous the first few years, but fortunately the local native tribe helped them and set them on a path toward using new food items. The Puritans are not to be confused with the Pilgrims. They were also a staunch religious group, founders of the Massachusetts Bay Colony at Boston in 1630, ten years after the Pilgrims landed at Plymouth. They were not a breakaway group, but rather had a royal charter for their colony. Both groups were essentially intolerant of any dissent, and the Puritans actually helped create Rhode Island in 1636 by driving out its founder Roger Williams from Massachusetts. By 1691, Massachusetts had expanded into the Connecticut River Valley, uniting both the Pilgrim and Puritan colonies and absorbing Maine.

One of the most notorious elements of early Massachusetts history was the witch trials in Salem in the late 1600's, where several women accused of witchcraft were put to death. Today the Witch Museum in Salem is a popular tourist destination. Salem is located on the northern fringe of metropolitan Boston and is easy to visit for anyone interested in its rather sordid history. And what is still puzzling to this day is the fact that the Ouija Board, a supposed means of contacting the spirit world, is manufactured by Parker Brothers, but their factory is located in Salem. Is there a connection or is it coincidence?

The American Revolutionary War actually began in Massachusetts, first with the Boston Massacre in 1770, the Boston Tea Party in 1773 and finally with the British and Americans exchanging fire at Lexington and Concord in 1775, the notorious shots heard around the world, as that incident became known. Many important battles were fought in Boston. Such famous events as the Battle of Bunker Hill and the Siege of Boston are still studied by American students to this day. And when you visit Boston, the locations for all of these battles become a reality. This further emphasizes the importance of reviewing the city's history prior to visiting.

Many leaders such as Samuel Adams, John Hancock and John Adams were Bostonians who came to the front as leaders in the fight for independence. John Adams became America's second president after George Washington. In the early years of the new nation, Shay's Rebellion in Massachusetts between 1786 and 1787 helped lead to the adoption of a strong constitution rather than the initially weak Articles of Confederation that first governed the country.

By the 19th century, the region surrounding Boston began to industrialize, with textiles being the major driving force. Fine quality shoes, kitchen ware and other former craft items began to be produced for the nation on a larger scale. This industrialization would ultimately lead to factory jobs that would be filled by a steady influx of immigrants, especially from Ireland and Italy. To this day, Boston's Irish and Italian communities are very strong. The famous Kennedy Family that produced one president and two senators along with other regional officials descended from early Irish immigrants to Boston.

During the 19th century, the greater Boston area produced such noted figures as Horace Mann with his progressive educational model, Henry David Thoreau and Ralph Waldo Emerson, two of the country's greatest philosophical poets. And in the early 20th century came the beloved poet Robert Frost.

During the lead up to the Civil War, Massachusetts was the most outspoken state against slavery. Such notables as John Brown and Frederick Douglass were citizens of Massachusetts. And during the Civil War, Massachusetts trained an all-Black regiment, the nation's first.

In the early 20th century, industrial activity in Massachusetts began to decline. The Great Depression followed by World War II saw a shift in the production of textiles, shoes and other fine quality goods now being produced in the Midwest and Southeast because of lower labor costs and more room for expansion. Today Massachusetts is more oriented toward high-tech industries, research and pharmaceuticals. The Boston area is today a major center of finance, commerce and higher education. Great universities such as Harvard, Massachusetts Institute of Technology, Radcliffe, Boston University, Clark and Boston College all have global recognition as prestigious institutions. There are also many medical facilities such as Harvard Medical and Brigham and Women's Hospital that have also garnered worldwide importance. The city is also home to many major banks, financial institutions and insurance companies.

CRUISE SHIP TERMINAL: Boston has a very large cruise ship terminal located approximately two kilometers or 1.5 miles from the downtown core.

The terminal is an elongated building with several reception and baggage stations since it supports numerous cruise lines. At any given time there can be two to three medium to large size cruise ships docked at the Boston terminal. The facilities are pretty basic and the entire facility can use a major makeover and remodeling. Motor coaches, taxis and tour busses line the curb in front of this massive building that stretches for approximately almost a kilometer in length.

A close up aerial of downtown Boston, (Work of Dave Wilson, CC BY SA 2.0, Wikimedia.org)

THE PHYSICAL LAYOUT OF BOSTON: The natural landscape is essentially flat, as Boston has few hills of any significance. The city developed on a small peninsula of land jutting into the bay, and the Charles River formed its northern boundary. As Boston and its sister city of Cambridge grew, the Charles River was dammed to widen it into a lake, which today is the cornerstone of the city. They bay is also quite irregular in shape with many smaller coves and inlets breaking up the shoreline. There are also numerous small rivers feeding into the bay, further breaking up the landscape.

Once all of the surrounding countryside was thickly wooded in a mix of deciduous trees and conifers. But most of it was turned into productive farmland by the time of the Revolutionary War, however, many small wooded areas were left, especially along the many streams and rivers flowing into the bay.

Many small villages developed during colonial times and they all are characterized by their small parade ground known as a commons and by their white timber churches. The commons was important in colonial times, as this is where the local militia would train since British troops were not there to protect the colonists from native hostilities or animal predation.

A map of the heart of Boston, (© OpenStreetMap contributors)

A general rule of thumb for understanding Boston is to say that the street pattern is chaotic. There is no single grid for greater Boston, with many streets running at angles, curving to conform to the old wagon trails from which they grew, or ending in "T" intersections. It is safe to say that Boston streets run ever way but straight for any distance. Only in Back Bay did some semblance of a grid pattern develop during the 19th century when streets were laid out parallel to one another facing to the Charles River.

Remember that this is the oldest large city in the United States and given its intense historic significance, it was difficult for any modicum of redevelopment of the street pattern to have taken place without having eliminated many important landmarks. Boston's overall layout is more like old European cities than the rest of the United States.

The heart of downtown Boston is known as The Boston Commons, and it is the largest of the municipal parade grounds where the militia once trained, as was true in all early New England communities. Today it is a large central park that has become the heart of Boston in more ways than just being a large mid-city park. This is a park with a long and colorful history.

At one time there was an elevated expressway that ran along the Boston waterfront just along the east side of the historic downtown core. It was a total eye sore, and underneath the roadway there were often vagrants camped out, mounds of garbage and other unsavory elements. And it was not very safe to walk from the waterfront into the heart of downtown Boston. It took many years of upheaval during what was called "The Big Dig," to create a tunnel through the heart of the city in which the expressway now runs. Above at street level, the former eye sore was turned into the Rose Kennedy Expressway, a beautiful park belt that separates a line of elegant office buildings, hotels and eateries from the rest of the downtown core. Actually rather than separating, it has brought them together into one integrated community. Today the waterfront, the North End and downtown merge into one viable district that is quite vibrant.

The modern downtown Boston skyline

A portion of the park that covers the Rose Kennedy Expressway Tunnel through the center of Boston

Most of residential Boston outside of the inner city core consists of wood houses and small apartment blocks, with brick reserved for larger buildings such as schools, clinics and churches. But in the inner city, brick tends to be the primary building material.

Boston is also a city of distinct neighborhoods some of which are politically separate communities, as the City of Boston comprises less than 30 percent of the total metropolitan area. Many visitors will recognize the importance of many of these neighborhoods. The most noted are:

* **North Boston** - This area, which is best identified by the Old North Church so identified with the famous ride of Paul Revere, is primarily the old immigrant Italian neighborhood. Initially it was one of the first residential areas to be settled and developed during the Colonial Era. But as the city grew, this neighborhood became home to mid and late 19th century immigrants mainly from Italy. There is a lot of local color, and good flavor in the many restaurants of North Boston.

North Boston is an Italian neighborhood and home to the Old North Church

* **South Boston** - This area is the core of the old immigrant Irish neighborhood. It was made famous by an old television sitcom called "Cheers." Few tourists visit South Boston except for those who were fans of the TV series.

* **Back Bay** is an area of landfill located south of the Boston Commons that developed with a heavy use of brownstone townhouses. It is today a very fashionable inner city district noted for its boutiques, galleries and eateries. This is one of the most expensive inner city neighborhoods, easy walking distance from most major downtown hotels.

* **Beacon Hill** is one of the oldest colonial neighborhoods in the city. Here the older brick houses on narrow, often cobbled, streets date back to the early 18th century. Beacon Hill is adjacent to the Boston Commons and the Massachusetts State House.

* **Charlestown**, located across the harbor from the city core is best known for the great battle of Bunker Hill fought during the Revolutionary War. The famous USS Ironside is docked along the waterfront of Charlestown.

* **Cambridge** is a separate city located north of the Charles River just across from Back Bay. This is a major suburb but it has a rich colonial history and excellent examples of 18th and 19th century architecture. It is home to Harvard University, Massachusetts Institute of Technology and Radcliff College.

WHAT TO SEE WHEN VISITING BOSTON:
Most ship itineraries devote an entire day to Boston, many staying until late evening. In all honesty a single day of eight to 10 hours in Boston does not even begin to allow enough time to absorb what this city has to offer in the way of its history, its distinctive charm and overall ambiance.

And as noted before, for some cruise lines, Boston is the port of embarkation or termination for the fall cruises into eastern Canada. In those instances, it is possible for guests to arrive in or depart from Boston several days before or after their cruise, enabling them to see more of the city and its surroundings. Boston is one of the most popular cities in the country, and a single day's port call only scratches the surface of what there is to see and do. Therefore, if your cruise embarks from or terminates in Boston, I strongly recommend as a minimum stay at least two full days, preferably more.

Boston is a large metropolitan region, and its population is over 4,600,000 residents. It is a congested city because in the inner heart of Boston the street pattern is still based upon the old streets laid out during Colonial times while the city was growing. Of all the cities in the country, Boston's lack of a uniform street pattern makes it the most complex of cities in which to navigate when going out on your own. It is very easy to get turned around and quickly lost in Boston, so a map is vital. Even with a good map, you will still find it a bit daunting to find your way around this city because of its many small streets that do not follow a common alignment. And traffic in the inner city is one of the worst in the country with regard to the commonly called gridlock, meaning that traffic can come to a complete standstill for many minutes at a time.

HOW TO EXPLORE THE CITY:
There are numerous ways to explore Boston, which are explained below:

* **Ship sponsored tours** are offered on those cruises spending the day in the city. These tours may be either by motor coach and/or walking or combining the two. For those who want to simply be guided and who do not mind being crowded together in a motor coach, this is a good way to explore the major highlights of the city. Some tours to famous sites outside of the city such as Lexington, Concord, Walden Pond and Salem are offered by various cruise lines.

* If your cruise begins or ends in Boston, some cruise lines offer a combination hotel and sightseeing package for pre or post cruise sightseeing. These can be single day tours around the city or longer tours including the famous Revolutionary War sites such as Lexington and Concord.

* **Car and driver** sightseeing can be arranged through your cruise line when the ship will be in the city for the day. Or if you are staying in a hotel for pre or post cruise sightseeing, most hotel concierges can make such arrangements. There is one exclusive company that offers excellent one on one sightseeing around the Boston area by private car. Check their web page at *www.trailblazertoursboston.com* for details.

* **Renting a car** - I personally do not recommend this option. Boston is complex with regard to its lack of a street pattern, it is congested and parking in the inner city is very limited, if not impossible.

* **Hop on hop off bus** - These trolley busses do provide good coverage of the inner city, stopping at the majority of famous landmarks, but as with all travel on the surface around the city, the busses are subject to the whims of traffic congestion. For details visit *www.hop-on-hop-off-bus.com/boston-bus-tours* for details and prices.

* **Boston "T"** - The "T" is short for the Boston subway system. It enables you to travel farther out from the city center and visit important sites. Maps are available locally to help you navigate the system. Although you will see little or nothing depending upon the line, as some do run at ground level, you do have the advantage of not being stuck in traffic on the underground lines. On those lines that do run at street level you can at least get some perspective of the city while en route.

For example to visit the campus of Harvard University, which is a popular destination, and then be able to walk around, it is best to take the Red Line and get off at Harvard Yard and explore both the university and Cambridge.

The "T" also extends south and visitors can use it to visit Plymouth Rock. The lines on the "T" are for the most part rather old but they do offer an excellent way to navigate the city.

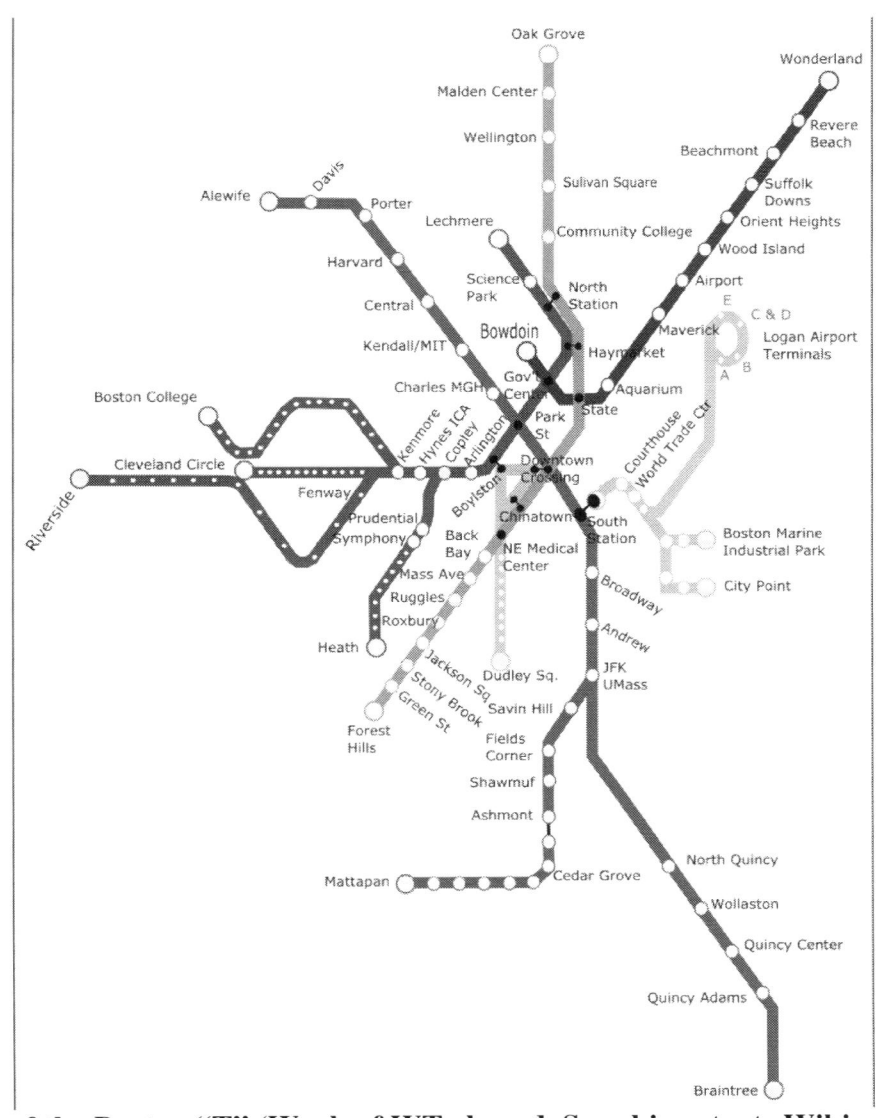

Map of the Boston "T" (Work of WT-shared, Sapphire at wts Wikivoyage, CC BY SA 3.0, Wikimedia.org)

* **Walking the Freedom Trail** - This specially marked trail that begins in front of the Massachusetts State House takes you through the old city, up through North Boston, over to Charleston and Bunker Hill and back through Beacon Hill, giving those who love to walk a good look at the city's Colonial history. You can walk all or a part of the Freedom Trail and see so much of the Colonial and Revolutionary War history of Boston, which is so interwoven with the downtown area.

* **Walking** the downtown core is another option if you are staying in a downtown hotel. There are many small churches, cemeteries and other interesting sites woven through the downtown such as the famous Quincy Market and the Boston Commons.

* Commuter rail - Beyond the immediate metro area, there are commuter trains that can take you out of Boston to visit places such as Salem, Gloucester and Cape Cod. You would most likely not be using the commuter rail system to visit these out of town destinations unless you are staying in Boston for several days, but the option does present itself.

WHAT TO SEE AND DO: Be aware that as a major city with a very diverse population, crime in Boston does exist but it is not as dominant a factor as in more industrialized eastern cities. Pickpockets are to be found in crowded venues, and also on the "T." Also be vigilant when out at night in the central city with regard to keeping your valuables safe. And do not dress in an ostentatious manner, as that only draws attention. Always be aware of your surroundings. Boston is not what I would call a dangerous city for the most part, but you do need to be careful and not stand out as a bewildered tourist.

The major sights that are must see venues, shown alphabetically:

Back Bay, (Work of Beyond my Ken, CC BY SA 4.0, Wikimedia.org)

* **Back Bay** - Built on landfill, this neighborhood of townhouses is one of the more inner city historic and upmarket districts. It is highly sought after by professionals who work in the downtown core. Newbury Street in Back Bay is noted for its fine shops and art galleries. Back Bay is characterized by row after row of brick townhouses.

Back Bay is an example of 19th century suburban expansion and today the brownstone row houses in this district are highly valued. Walking the streets of Back Bay gives the visitor a totally different feel for Boston than Beacon Hill or North Boston. There are also several important high rise buildings in Back Bay, most notable being the Prudential Building.

* **Beacon Hill** – This is one of the oldest and most famous residential districts in any American colonial city. It is only a slightly elevated hill and it is located just to the north of the Massachusetts State House. This neighborhood contains very narrow streets, mostly cobbled and the old houses date back for the most part to the Colonial Era. It is considered a prized neighborhood by Bostonians and real estate is very costly.

Beacon Hill is an historic residential area dating to Colonial times

* **Boston Commons** - This large park was once the parade ground for the Colonial militia. Every city and town of Colonial vintage has its common. The Boston Common is in the heart of the city and is a great place to just observe the general daily flow of life. It is not recommended to walk in the Commons after dark. Hours are from 7 AM to 9 PM.

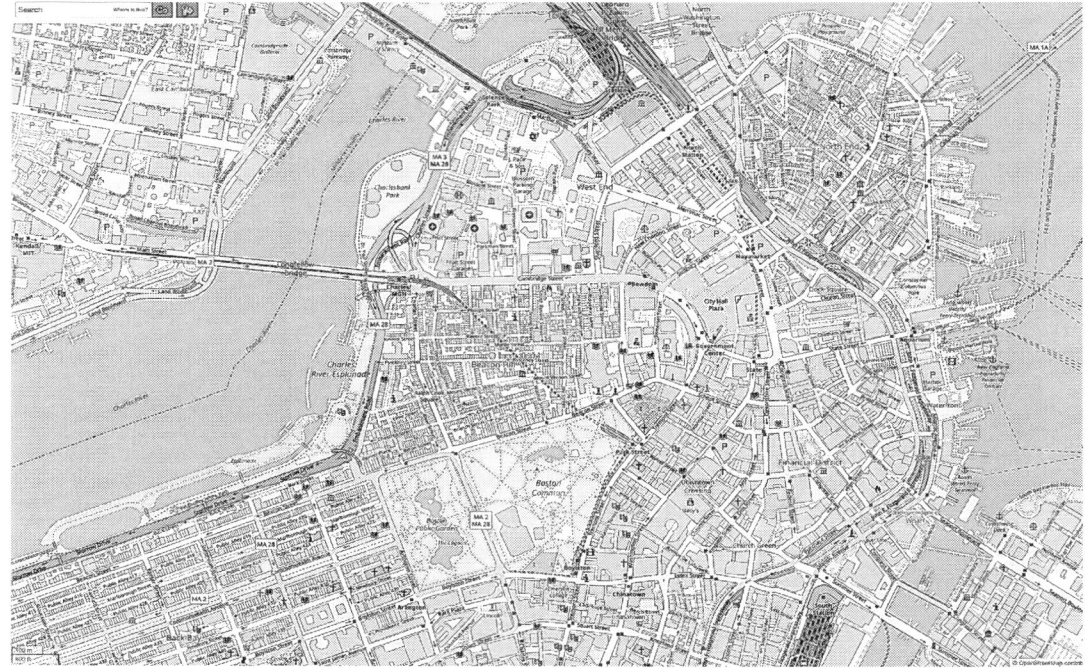

Map of downtown Boston, (© OpenStreetMap contributors)

* **Boston Tea Party Museum and Ship** - The museum and ship commemorate the Boston Tea Party, however, they are not located on the original site. Today it is located at 308 Congress Street. It is open from 10 AM to 5 PM. Tours are given during these hours.

* **Faneuil Hall Marketplace** - This once daily farmer's market is today simply an open air marketplace with a variety of items and crafts being sold. It is a very historic and popular venue. Located at 1 Faneuil Hall Square, it is open from 10 AM to 9 PM daily and Noon to 6 PM on Sunday.

* **Fenway Park** - The most beloved baseball stadium in America, Fenway Park is best seen if a home game is being played. Generally by the time of the fall cruises, the regular season has wound down. But if Boston is in the playoffs, and if you are a baseball fan, you need to go on line and try and get tickets. When no games are played there are tours offered of this famous stadium.

Tours are offered between 9 AM and 5 PM. For more information visit their web page at www.mlb.com/redsocks/ballpark for details.

In the heart of downtown Boston with Macy's on the right

* **First Church of Christ Scientist** - This massive and elegant church of the Christian Science faith is quite a major Boston landmark. It is in the Back Bay area at 210 Massachusetts Avenue and a definite must see building with its magnificent grounds. Group tours are given NOON to 4 PM Tuesday, 1 to 4 PM Wednesday, NOON to 5 PM Thursday thru Saturday and 11 AM to 3 PM Sunday.

* **Freedom Trail** - This is the most popular walk in Boston, as it shows you so many of the historic sights, some of which are individually noted below. But it is the overall walk that is the treat because it shows you the city. The trail begins in front of the Massachusetts State House facing onto the Boston Commons. To download a map of the trail, visit www.thefreedomtrail.org . A visit to Boston is really not complete unless you walk the Freedom Trail. To visit all the historic venues listed on the map can take an entire day, and it is because of the city's long and illustrious history that I recommend staying over in Boston if your cruise either begins or terminates here. For one day cruise visits it is hard to get more than a cursory overview of the city.

Along the Freedom Trail at the Old South Meeting House

* **Harvard University** - Take the Red Line of the "T" to Harvard Square and you are in the heart of Cambridge. The University campus is essentially all around you. It is a massive campus, and just to walk around and feel the ambiance of this venerable institution of higher learning is worth the effort. Harvard is one of the two oldest universities in the United States, founded in 1636. The campus presents a mix of old colonial, 18th and 19th century buildings plus a few modern additions.

Ratcliff College is attached to Harvard University and affiliated with it. Ratcliff began in 1879, making it a prestigious tertiary institution established for women.

* **Haymarket** – This is still the city's large outdoor green market where farmers bring their fresh produce to sell to city residents. It is very colorful and has a flavor all its own. There is a strong immigrant component to the merchants in Haymarket, which adds to its color, sights and sounds. It is located at 100 Hanover Street. It is open weekdays from 8 AM to 8 PM and Saturday from 8 AM to 7 PM. Sunday hours are from 10 AM to 8 PM. You should visit early in the morning to get the full impact of the activity that is so vibrant.

* **John F. Kennedy Presidential Library** - This is one of the most popular venues in the city, located on Columbia Point and open daily 9 AM to 5 PM, closed on major public holidays. It would be necessary to go as part of a guided tour, via the Hop on hop off bus or take a taxi, as the "T" does not come close to it. Some cruise lines staying in Boston for a full day offer a special tour.

* **Massachusetts State House** – Located at the top end of the Boston Commons, this iconic building with its golden dome is the legislative center for the Commonwealth of Massachusetts. The state house faces on to the Boston Commons and thus unlike other state capitol buildings, it does not have any significant grounds.

Tours of the state capitol are offered on weekdays from 10 AM to 3:45 PM at no charge.

Massachusetts State House

* **Museum of Fine Art** - This is one of the country's most celebrated museum collections and if you love art, plan to spend several hours. It is located at 465 Huntington Avenue some distance from the city center. It can be reached via the "T" on the Orange Line at Ruggles Station. It opens at 10 AM and is open until 5 PM daily with extended hours to 9 PM Wednesday thru Friday.

* **North Boston** - On the Freedom Trail, North Boston is an old, historic part of the city that became home to Italian immigrants. And sitting in the middle of it is The Old North Church.

* **Old North Church** - This small church is located in the heart of North Boston and it has a steeple that is very easy to recognize. It was from the top that a signal would be given to Paul Revere in 1775 to warn the outlying areas that the British were coming. One of by land and two if by sea was the code. And history tells us that Paul Revere then set out to warn the people in Lexington and Concord. This church is a very memorable part of Americana. It is open from 9 AM to 6 PM daily during the fall.

* **Old South Meeting House** – Along the Freedom Trail, this is one of the many important historic sites to visit. This old congregational church is where the organizers of the Boston Tea Party met to plan their raid. It is open daily from 10 AM to 4 PM.

The Old South Meeting House on Washington Street

* **Prudential Center** – Prudential Center is one of two tallest buildings in downtown Boston. It is prominently located in Back Bay at 800 Boylston Street and open from 10 AM to 9 PM. The observation deck provides you with one of the best high altitude views of all of greater Boston. But make sure it is a clear day before going.

* **Quincy Market** - Located at 4 South Market Street and open well into the night, this once daily farmer's market is today simply a gallery of take away food, but of high quality. Much of what is sold is traditional to the Boston food scene. Although quite frenetic, many visitors like to partake of the various seafoods and other delicacies offered. Table space is often difficult to get, so many people simply take their order outside and eat in the two plazas that border each side of the marketplace.

It is a very historic and popular venue. The market is open from 10 AM TO 9 PM and Noon to 6 PM on Sunday.

Quincy Market

Old Ironside, the USS Constitution

* **USS Constitution** - This strong wooden man of war became known as "Old Ironsides" because its hull was so thick and resistant to cannon fire. It is still commissioned as a United States Navy Vessel. It is a museum moored along the Freedom Trail in Charleston. It is open from 10 AM to 6 PM daily during the fall.

TOURING OUTSIDE OF BOSTON: There are still so many more venues within Boston, but I have covered the most major ones, and if you visited every site on my list above, you would spend several days. Outside of Boston there are many important sights, but I am listing only those I believe are the most significant and if you have only one day if your ship is just stopping in Boston, you would miss the entire city if you chose one of these visits that are shown below alphabetically:

* **House of Seven Gables** is another popular site to visit. It was built in 1668, and it featured prominently in the works of Nathaniel Hawthorne's novels *House of the Seven Gables* and *The Scarlet Letter.* The house is open daily from 10 AM to 5 PM. For anyone who read this classic story while in school a visit makes the House of Seven Gables come very much alive.

The house is open to visitors daily from 10 AM to 4 PM and is one of the highlights of visiting Salem.

The old North Bridge where the first shot of the American Revolutionary War was fired, the one "heard around the world"

* **Lexington and Concord** - Try and go on an organized tour as it is easier to see the important North Bridge where "the shot heard round the world" was fired to start the American Revolutionary War. Also the Minute Man National Historic Park is an important American treasure. The park is open from 8 AM to 6 PM and includes the entire area of the Battle of Lexington and Concord. I prefer the freedom of visiting with a car and driver despite the added expense, as it gives you more freedom to visit at your own pace.

* **Walden Pond State Reservation** - Located just outside of Concord, this is the site where Henry David Thoreau lived in his small cabin for two years contemplating life and society. His famous book *Walden* is a great American classic that once was required reading in public high schools. Most of us who were made to read the book while in high school could not fully appreciate its message, as *Walden* was never written with young school age children in mind. This is a powerful philosophical work.

The pond is open to visitors from 7:30 AM to 7 PM daily.

Walden Pond, (Work of Andrew Douglass, CC BY SA 3.0, Wikimedia.org)

* **Witch Dungeon Museum** located in the heart of Salem is the main venue when visiting, but it is a bit touristy. They put on a show that one might call a bit trite, but it does tell the story, which is a serious one. Open from 10 AM to 5 PM, located at 16 Lynde Street in the town center.

ACCOMMODATIONS:
If your tour embarks or terminates in Boston, as I noted previously, you should plan to stay for a few days. Boston is a city of many hotels and they vary greatly in quality. I only like to recommend five and four-star properties. I might be spoiled, but I believe every cruise should begin and end with the comfort, convenience and safety of a top hotel.

Boston is a major travel destination and offers a great array of hotels in the central part of the city that vary from budget to deluxe. All major brand names are to be found and for details I refer you to Trip Advisor where you will find objective ratings in every price and comfort category. Also consult with your cruise line, as quite often they will have negotiated pre or post cruise special rates.

Here are my personalized choices for Boston shown alphabetically:

* **Boston Harbor Hotel** - This is the most highly rated hotel in the city, located at 70 Rowes Wharf right in the heart of the choice Boston waterfront. This is definitely a five-star hotel providing all the amenities and services you would expect from such a property. There are two dining rooms, one specializing in seafood. The hotel offers full services including a concierge to help you with any touring arrangements. I GIVE IT *****

* **Boston Marriott at Long Wharf** - Located at 296 State Street, this four-star property is well respected for good service and convenience. It is in the heart of the most historic part of Boston. Do not expect five-star service, but likewise it does not charge five-star prices, but it does comfortably meet four-star standards. And the location is outstanding with most rooms having harbor views. Many attractions are close by with Quincy Market just across the parkway. And the "T" is adjacent. But it is a very fine hotel and so conveniently located to the majority of historic sites. I GIVE IT ****

* **Four Seasons Hotel** - As you would expect, this five-star property meets all of the standards you expect at Four Seasons. All amenities you expect from a five-star property are well represented in this property. The hotel is very convenient for doing walking tours of the city, as it is at 200 Boylston Street, facing the Boston Commons. It is hard to beat any Four Season Hotel for comfort and elegance. I GIVE IT *****

* **Hotel Commonwealth** - Located in Back Bay at 500 Commonwealth Avenue, it is a smaller five-star property and situated in more of a neighborhood setting with plenty of shops and restaurants around.

It does offer impeccable service and dining in what is generally thought of as a boutique atmosphere. I GIVE IT *****

* **Ritz Carlton Boston** – This Ritz Carlton is a superb five-star property overlooking the Boston Public Garden. It is located at 10 Avery Street and is very close to the major attractions in the city center and along the Freedom Trail.

The hotel offers a chic dining room, spa and fitness center, meeting facilities, concierge and all the amenities you expect in a five-star property. I GIVE IT *****

The Ritz Carlton overlooking the Public Garden

* **Seaport Boston Hotel** - Located at 1 Seaport Lane in a newly developing waterfront area just south of the city center. But it is very close to the cruise ship terminal. It is also very highly rated with a high degree of client satisfaction. And it provides all of the amenities you would expect. I GIVE IT ****

DINING OUT: A book on all the fine quality restaurants in Boston would be almost as large as this entire book. This is a city where dining out is an art form and Bostonians do like good food and evenings out on the town. Yes in some ways it is a "party town." But food is legendary in Boston and the city takes pride in its seafood, Italian and fine continental dining. In drawing up this list, I have chosen a handful of what I consider to be representative of the Boston food scene, with an emphasis upon its fresh seafood. Here are my choices shown alphabetically:

* **Atlantic Fish Company** – At 761 Boylston Street in Back Bay, this is another one of Boston's venerable seafood restaurants. Fresh oysters, tuna tartar, crab and lobster rolls and lobster omelets are among their many favorite dishes. They are open Monday thru Thursday from 11:30 AM to 11 PM, Friday and

Saturday from 11:30 AM to 11:30 PM and Sunday from 11 AM to 11 PM and reservations can be made by calling 617 267 4000.

* **Capital Grille** – At 900 Boylston Street in the Hynes Convention Center, this is a very elegant restaurant serving American cuisine and specializing in steak, but also having a full range of delicious menu items. The atmosphere and service are quite impeccable and the quality of the cuisine is excellent. They are open Monday thru Friday from 11:30 AM to 8 PM, Saturday from 5 to 8 PM and Sunday from 4 to 8 PM. Reservations should be made by calling 617 262 8900.

* **James Hook and Company** - At 15 Northern Avenue, open from 10 AM to 4 PM, with closing extended to 5 PM on Friday and Saturday. This is a great place for lunch. Their specialty is lobster, and remember Maine is not far away so the quality will be excellent. They are also noted for their lobster rolls as well as live lobster prepared to order. They do not accept reservations.

Legal Sea Food on Long Wharf

* **Legal Sea Food** - There are numerous locations around the central city, check with your hotel concierge for the one nearest you. If you are here for the day on a cruise port call, then the nearest one is at Long Wharf opposite the Marriott Hotel. Legal Seafood is a Boston legend, but some say it is not what it

once was. Reviews always show a high level of satisfaction, but not perfection, as some are disappointed. They do offer an incredible menu selection. Generally they are very crowded for lunch or dinner, so try going at the in between hour, say between 2 and 4 PM. Reservations are not accepted for small groups.

* **Mario's Restaurant** - This fine Italian restaurant is considered by many to be the best in Boston. Its menu is diverse and is genuine, not Americanized. It is a neighborhood type restaurant, open from 5:30 to 9:30 PM Monday thru Saturday with extended closing at 9 PM Friday and Saturday. They are located at 347 Chelsea Street across the harbor in upper East Boston. You will need to take a taxi, but it is well worthwhile. Call 617 567 8608 to see if they are taking reservations.

* **Mistral** – For elegant evening dining, Mistral at 223 Columbus Avenue is one of the most beautiful of French and Continental restaurants in Boston. The grandeur of the restaurant and the attentive service compliment a menu that is both diverse in its offerings and is definitely the hallmark of haute cuisine. The menu does also include vegetarian friendly dishes. Their hours of service are daily from 5:30 to 9:30 PM. Call them at 617 867 9300 to see if they are taking table reservations.

* **Ostra** - One of the most highly rated seafood restaurants in Boston, Ostra is located at 1 Charles Street in downtown. It is only open for dinner between 5:30 and 9:30 PM Tuesday thru Saturday. It has excellent ambiance and a wide variety of seafood offerings. Reservations are generally accepted through www.opentable.com.

* **Saltie Girl** – Located at 281 Dartmouth Street in Back Bay, this is a very popular and interesting seafood restaurant. They offer a very incredible and diverse menu of the freshest fish and seafood available. And they are also vegetarian friendly. Lobster rolls and fresh oysters are specialties. Their hours are open daily from 11 AM until 9 PM with a 10 AM opening on Sunday. Call 617267 0691 for table reservations.

* **Salumeria Italiana** - A venerable Italian restaurant at 151 Richmond Street in the traditional North Boston Italian district. I would say it is just as good as if you were in Italy, and they have many choices of regional specialties. They are open for both lunch and dinner Monday thru Saturday from 9 AM to 5 PM.. They are essentially more of an Italian grocery but do serve prepared dishes for on-site dining. No reservations are taken.

SHOPPING: Downtown Boston was once a major shopping Mecca, but the two great department stores that were so much a part of the retail scene are gone. However, there is a quite large Macy's located on Washington Street that offers a broad selection of merchandise. There are also the major suburban shopping malls you would expect to find in a city the size of Boston, but most people can find the same shopping at home. What I recommend below are those shops that offer fine quality local crafts and fine arts, catering to the tastes of visitors:

* **Faneuil Hall Marketplace** - Located at 1 Faneuil Hall Square adjacent to Faneuil Hall and Quincy Market offers a great variety of local crafts and traditional souvenir items. This area is heavily patronized by visitors to Boston and it has everything from typical kitsch to quality handmade craft items. The hall is open daily from 10 AM to 9 PM and most shops do observe those hours.

* **Haymarket** - This is the outdoor farmer's market that is so European in flavor, and it runs for blocks. You will not really be shopping other than possibly for some fruit or goodies to take back to the ship or your hotel. It centers on Blackstone Street right near Faneuil Hall. The hours of operation are Monday thru Friday from 8 AM to 8 PM, Saturday from 8 AM to 7 PM and Sunday from 10 AM to 8 PM.

* **Macy's** – Located at 450 Washington Street, this is the largest full service department store in Boston and one of the largest stores in the chain. It caters to a wide diversity of tastes and price ranges. Hours of service are weekdays from 10 AM to 10 PM Saturday from 9 AM to 10 PM and Sunday from 10 AM to 9 PM.

* **Newbury Street** - In Back Bay this major street is noted primarily for its art galleries offering a variety of national and international artists. There are also loads of boutiques on this fashionable street. Most maintain normal working hours between 10 AM and 6 PM, but some do stay open into the evening hours.

* **Prudential Center** - In Back Bay at 800 Boylston Street, the shopping arcade offers quite a variety of major national brand name stores. The center is open daily from 10 AM to 9 PM and most shops observe those hours.

FINAL NOTES: There is so much more than can be said about Boston, but even if you are staying a few days, you will only just begin to get to know this complex city. When surveys are done of the livability of American cities, Boston is always one of the highest ranking of the major cities in the country.

Visually it is rather drab because of the inner city being so heavily into the use of brick and stone, and it is very congested. Suburban Boston consists of mile after mile of wood houses, but still in many neighborhoods the density is quite high. But it is the lifestyle that gives this city its charm and popularity.

Boston is both steeped in American history, but also a city pressing forward, as can be seen by its growing downtown skyline. The downtown area is not in any way losing ground to the suburbs. Yes in retail shopping, it is not what it once was. But with the importance of tourism, and with the ongoing modernization and new construction, downtown is still lively and safe for visitors.

NEW YORK CITY, NEW YORK

A map of greater New York City, (© OpenStreetMap contributors)

New York City is affectionately known as "The Big Apple" and its fame is worldwide. Until the middle of the 20th century it was considered to be the world's largest city, however, there are many Asian and Latin American cities whose population has surpassed it, but there is still one New York City. This chapter will not be an in depth look at New York City since the focus of this book is on fall cruising the waters of Eastern Canada and New England. But I cannot ignore New York City because the vast majority of the fall cruises either begin or terminate at the cruise terminal along the Hudson River in Manhattan. And because New York City is an iconic venue among world cities, most cruisers will either spend one or more days at the start or conclusion of their cruise visiting this most exciting of American cities. This chapter is intended as a bonus to the book to provide those unfamiliar with visiting New York City some basic information on accommodation, sightseeing and dining. The chapter is in no way intended to be a detailed account of what the city offers since there are literally hundreds of New York City guidebooks on the market.

WELCOME TO NEW YORK CITY: New York City is the largest city in the United States with a metropolitan area population as defined by the United States Census Bureau includes suburbs in Connecticut, New Jersey and extending into Pennsylvania, but excluding Philadelphia is over 20,000,000. By world standards most sources consider it to be the eighth largest urban area in the world, but not all lists are in agreement. If we go back to the year 1900, London was the world's largest city, but following World War II, New York City emerged as the number one city in population. Since the late decades of the 20th century, population in many east Asian cities and those in Latin America have exploded while New York City has remained relatively stable. Tokyo is the largest urban center in the world today with over 35,000,000 in its metropolitan area and Mexico City is said to be the largest city in the Western Hemisphere. But New York City is still recognized worldwide as an iconic city, and it is the most visited and venerated by tourists around the globe. Unfortunately in this new century, it has also become one of the most vulnerable target among terrorists, as witnessed by September 11, 2001, a date burned into world memory.

An incredible aerial on take-off from La Guardia over Manhattan looking south along the Hudson River

THE NATURAL LANDSCAPE: The Hudson River is an important waterway whose tributaries rise in upstate New York in the Adirondack Mountains with smaller tributaries draining east from the Catskill Mountains closer to the Atlantic Coastal Plain. The Upper Hudson and Mohawk Rivers converge to form a wide and deep river channel that flows south into the soft glacial plain close to the sea. At the end of the great Ice Age or Pleistocene, the retreating continental glacier stalled for thousands of years that enabled a long sinuous ridge of debris to form, creating what would become Long Island when sea level ultimately rose. This island, which is over 160 kilometers or 100 miles long, forms a part of New York City with two of its major boroughs named Queens and Brooklyn having developed at the western edge of the island. The southern shore is low and marshy with numerous lagoons protected by think sand bars. Jamaica Bay is where JFK International Airport is located.

Lower Manhattan seen from the ship on an evening sail out

The Hudson River scoured out a channel between the low lying marshes to its west after flowing alongside a line of cliffs marking higher ground and a narrow peninsula of land to the east separating the river from Long Island. And a narrow channel was formed to help drain some of the river water out into a massive bay. This channel is today called the East River and it cut off the lower tip of the narrow peninsula, creating the Island of Manhattan. Farther to the southeast, another channel draining out to sea cut off a piece of land that today is known as Staten Island.

The changes in tidal bores four times a day further scoured this estuary, creating what is today recognized as New York Harbor, one of the most sheltered anchorages on the Atlantic Coast. And it was this harbor combined with the Hudson-Mohawk River that created a corridor inland toward the Great Lakes and set the stage for the growth of a major port city.

Originally the land was covered with a mix of grassy marshes with clusters of broadleaf trees growing on the higher ground. Many of these wooded areas ultimately became urban parks or home to placid suburban communities that took advantage of the woodland environment.

New York City has a transitional climate that goes from warm to hot, humid summers to cold and blustery winters that can experience fierce storms known as a Nor'easter, which can bring heavy snow to the urban landscape. And in recent years with climate change being a major factor, New York City has seen several Atlantic hurricanes penetrate this far north, causing damage that was never anticipated.

A VERY BRIEF HISTORY: It is vital to know how New York City grew to the great metropolis it is today even if you are only planning to stay for a day or two. How can you appreciate what you are seeing without understanding how it came to be?

This brief chronology of New York City will help you understand the basics relating to how the mouth of the Hudson River developed into one of the world's most famous cities. In reading this brief history you can discount the favorite myth that the Europeans bought Manhattan for a few trinkets and coins. Although it is a popular story told to children, there is no documented evidence of this occurring.

The first European known to have sailed into New York Harbor was Giovanni da Verranzano, sailing under the French flag, entered the narrows in 1524. If that name is familiar it is because the present day entry into the harbor is spanned by the Verranzano Narrows Bridge.

In 1609, one year after Ville de Québec was founded Henry Hudson explored the river now named in his honor. And Samuel de Champlain discovered the large lake between New York and Vermont now named for him.

It was the Netherlands that established a settlement on Manhattan Island in 1624, naming it Nieuw Amsterdam. And they held control for four decades until the British captured it in 1664 and renamed it in honor of the Duke of York.

Several battles were fought in upstate New York and Vermont during the French and Indian War between 1754 and 1763 for control of the valuable corridor of the Hudson River Valley leading into the interior, but the city was not openly contested.

In 1765, the first conference of colonial leaders was held in New York City precipitated by the hated British Stamp Act. This was the first prelude to ultimate revolution.

In 1775, Ethan Allen, Benedict Arnold and the Green Mountain Boys, a Vermont militia group, managed to capture Fort Ticonderoga on Lake Champlain without violence and this was a major victory, securing the Hudson River Corridor against the British.

In 1776, New York joined twelve other colonies to declare their independence and proclaim a new nation. One year later, the colony adopted a constitution and George Clinton became its first governor. The Battle of Saratoga was fought four months later, considered today by many historians as the most important victory in the early years of the war, leading the joining of forces with the French and their famous General Lafayette.

In November of 1783, General George Washington made a triumphant entry into New York City on the heels of the British military departure, as the Revolutionary War was drawing close to its conclusion. As the most strategically located city, it became the first capital of the new nation. And in 1789, George Washington took the presidential oath at Federal Hall, where his famous statue now stands at 26 Wall Street. New York City remained the capital of the nation until 1790 when Congress moved to Philadelphia in anticipation of the completion of Washington City. Wall Street continues as a major financial hub, as the first stock exchange opened there in 1792.

Despite its strategic location, the capital of the State of New York was located in Albany because of its proximity to the confluence of the Mohawk and Hudson Rivers. And in 1802, the United States Military Academy was founded south of Albany at a bend in the Hudson River known as West Point.

The Hudson River was the key to travel by barge into the interior beyond the Appalachian Mountains and in 1807, Robert Fulton's steamboat made the journey north to Albany. This ushered in a totally new mode of transport. But it was the opening of the Erie Canal in 1825 that enabled barges to connect New York City with Lake Erie. This was an even more significant event because it secured the city as the most preeminent port on the Atlantic Seaboard.

The first New York native to become President was Martin Van Buren, sworn into office in 1837. In 1850, Millard Filmore, also born in New York State became President of the United States. Theodore Roosevelt became President in 1901. Franklin Roosevelt, the longest serving president, took his first oath of office in 1933. Donald Trump became President in 2016.

In 1863, Long Island and Manhattan Island were connected by the newly opened Brooklyn Bridge. In its day it was considered to be a marvel of design and engineering. It still stands today and is one of the most iconic of symbols of the city along with the Empire State Building, which came seven decades later.

To commemorate the centennial of American Independence, the Statue of Liberty was dedicated on a small island in the Hudson River estuary. It has without question become the symbol of America. As our first partner in the struggle for independence, the statue was a gift from France.

The Statue of Liberty – quintessential symbol of a nation

Between the 1890's and the 1930's, New York City saw over 12,000,000 immigrants enter the country through the Ellis Island facility adjacent to the Statue of Liberty. Today both sites are national historic monuments and World Heritage Sites, visited by almost all who come to the city.

In 1901, Theodore Roosevelt, a New York City native, was sworn in as President of the United States upon the assassination of William McKinley, which occurred in Buffalo, New York.

In 1902, the skyline of New York City, which today is the symbol of the skyscraper, saw the first such building completed. The Flatiron Building on lower Fifth Avenue is now dwarfed by a forest of high rises, but at 22-stories, it was an amazing structure in its day. Two years later, another marvel occurred with the opening of the first subway line. The present subway system is still one of the five largest in the world, but no longer number one.

In 1931 three engineering marvels were opened to the public. First came the Chrysler Building, the world's tallest at its dedication. A few months later, the Empire State Building was opened and it remained the world's tallest until 1974 when the Sears Tower in Chicago captured the record. Today there are numerous structures still taller. The CN Tower in Toronto is now the tallest structure in the Western Hemisphere.

In 1933, Franklin D. Roosevelt, born along the Hudson River, became the 32nd President of the United States and held office until his death at the start of his fourth term.

The 1939 World's Fair in New York City showcased so many great marvels of the day, but soon its peaceful intent was overshadowed on September 1st when Nazi Germany invaded Poland, touching off World War II.

In 1952, the United Nations located in New York City and its headquarters building, standing along the East River, is one of the city's iconic buildings.

September 11th, 2001 has now been etched into the collective memory of the world as another day to quote the late President Franklin D. Roosevelt that "will live in infamy" along with Pearl Harbor.

In 2016, Donald J. Trump became President of the United States, becoming the fifth New York native to be sworn into that office.

I think you can see from this very brief history that New York City has played a dynamic role in the growth of the nation. It continues to be the financial hub of the country, the center of publishing, center of the performing arts, the most international of cities and holder of so many other firsts. No city in the country is as important as New York City.

THE LAYOUT OF NEW YORK CITY: Given its fragmentation by waterways and its lack of a single cohesive grid pattern, New York City has a very complex makeup that is confusing to visitors. My suggestion is for you to not even consider renting a car and driving yourself. It is a most congested city and with such a complex street pattern, as a visitor you will regret attempting to drive. As the motto of one of the old motor coach companies, "leave the driving to us," you need to use public transit or have a car and driver if you choose not to take organized tours.

The city is divided into semi-autonomous boroughs, the most famous and most visited being Manhattan Island. The borough of Bronx occupies the mainland peninsula north of Manhattan. Queens and Brooklyn occupy the northwestern and southwestern ends of Long Island respectively. And the borough of Richmond occupies Staten Island. Bridges, tunnels and ferries connect the various boroughs and also join the heavily populated New Jersey suburbs to the city.

EXPLORING THE CITY: New York City takes days to explore and most cruise passengers will only spend one or two days maximum either before or after their cruise. My recommendations for exploring the city are as follows:

* If you are on a pre or post cruise package, you will no doubt have an all-day motor coach excursion booked for you. This will show you the basic sights of the city. And then if you have time left over you can easily walk in the vicinity of your hotel, as most that are chosen by the cruise lines are in the midtown area close to the lower end of Central Park and also within walking distance of Times Square.

* If you have chosen to stay in the city on your own, I recommend that you take a motor coach tour around the city to see the major highlights. The most recommended of the full tours, not the type you hop on and off, is a company called Small Bus Tours. Check their web page at *www.smallbustoursnyc.com* for full details.

* **WAYS TO GET AROUND THE CITY:** Here are the various ways to get around New York City since I do not recommend renting a car for sightseeing. Apart from the congestion and the need to follow maps or GPS, parking is one of the most difficult of factors in having a car of your own. My suggestions are:

A map of the heart of New York city, (© OpenStreetMap contributors)

* **Private car and driver** is one way to be able to explore the city with privacy and comfort. You can tailor your itinerary to your own taste. Most hotel concierge desks can arrange this option for you. If you wish to arrange this on your own I recommend Tours by Locals, which is a very good program. Visit on line at www.toursbylocals.com/New-York-City-Tours .

* **Hop on hop off bus tours** are the most popular way to get around to all the major city venues.. Here are the ones I recommend:

** The Hop on Hop off Bus Tours web page is *www.hop-on-hop-off-bus.com* where you will find a large number of different tours offered. And you can check the itineraries and prices for each tour.

** Skyline Sightseeing is another service. Check their web page for details at *www.skylinesightseeingny.com* .

** Also check out Gray Line Tours at *www.grayline.com* and key in New York City for full details.

Midtown west side low rise older apartment blocks

Uptown west side expensive high rise residential living

Food trucks abound in Manhattan

A homeless man in Central Park seems content with his lot in life

* **The New York City subway** system is very extensive with over 20 different lines. But it is crowded, not the safest means of transport and can be rather confusing for a visitor. And much of the system runs underground so you miss so much of the city when traveling between venues. I personally do not advise using the subway because it frankly gives you a less than desirable impression of the city.

* **Walking** is a great way to get around if you are staying at a major hotel in midtown Manhattan. It is a great way to enjoy the sights and it is also the healthiest way to explore, if you are capable.

MAJOR SIGHTS TO SEE: There are so many sights to be seen that even a recommended list will be exceptionally large. And with so many venues and people's individual tastes, I have limited my suggestions to just the most major venues that are an absolute must. My list is in no way to be a complete listing of the major venues, but most cruise passengers have limited time to spend, so just following my recommendations will take up at least two full days of sightseeing. Here are my limited choices shown alphabetically:

* **Brooklyn Bridge** – The most iconic bridge is the first major suspension bridge in the city. It was built in the early 1870's and spans the East River. Its two stone towers have a distinctive look that has been emulated many times.

You can walk across a special boardwalk above the traffic lanes. It is safe during the daytime, but not recommended for walking after dark. But it is a fairly long walk and unless you can flag down a taxi for the return to Manhattan it can be quite tiring to walk it both ways.

* **Central Park** – This is the largest park on Manhattan Island, a giant rectangle that extends from 59th Street north to 110th Street and from Central Park West to 5th Avenue on the east. It contains many important sights such as its lakes, playing fields, gardens and monuments. This is a great place for walking and getting amazing views of the Manhattan skyline.

The park is open from 6 AM to 1 AM daily, but it is not recommended for walking after dark. Even during the daytime there are minor incidents of pickpocketing and other non-violent crimes. Taking a horse drawn carriage through the park is one safe way of enjoying it.

* **Columbus Circle** – This busy monument marks the southwestern corner of Central Park and is an important circle where Broadway crosses 8th Avenue and 59th Street. It is surrounded by numerous famous buildings such as the towering Times Warner Center. This is one of those must see landmark street corners.

The famous world sculpture at Columbus Circle

* **Ellis Island** – Once the gateway for millions of immigrants, the site that processed them fell into disrepair. Today it is a museum under the National Park Service. For information on visiting the island as well as the Statue of Liberty visit on line with www.statueoflibertytickets.com/Ellis-island-Tour .

* **Empire State Building** – Although not the world's tallest now, the Empire State Building with its Art Deco design is still an iconic structure. It stands pretty much alone and is highly visible despite there being taller buildings close by. To visit the observation deck on a clear day is still considered to present one of the best views of the city. Located at 20 West 34th Street, the observation deck is open from 8 AM to 2 AM daily. The wait for an elevator can sometimes be long, but early morning is the best time to visit to avoid the crowds.

The Empire State Building at early evening seen from the Hudson River

* **Grand Central Station** – The world's most famous railway station located at 89 East 42nd Street, just a few blocks from Times Square, is another of the city's iconic buildings. Built in a Beaux Arts style, rather ornate and elegant, it served as the main station for interstate travel, but today is used strictly for commuter rail traffic. It is still one of the busiest stations in the country and at times is absolutely mobbed with commuters. It is one of those must see buildings, if nothing more than just a quick peek inside the main hall. The station first opened in 1913. Docent led tours are given daily between 9 AM and 6 PM. For further detail visit *www.grandcentralterminal.com* and click on to visit and then tours.

* **Greenwich Village** – Once the hub of the counterculture movement, this neighborhood in lower Manhattan is composed of small apartment blocks lining leafy green streets. Today it is home to hundreds of small restaurants, cafes, bars and clubs. The night life of the Village is still popular with young professionals. The heart of the Village is Washington Square Park. Again this is one of those must see districts of Manhattan. The Village is bounded by the Hudson River on the west, Broadway on the east and Houston Street on the south with 14th Street on the north. If you choose to use the subway during

daylight hours, it can be reached from the 8th Street Station on Broadway. I recommend a taxi rather than the subway.

* **Macy's Department Store** – Said to be the world's largest single store, this is the flagship store of the nationwide chain. It is quite an interesting place to visit and often you will find some great bargains in various departments.

Located at 34th Street and Broadway in Herald Square, it is open Monday thru Thursday from 10 AM to 10 PM, Friday until 11 PM and Saturday it opens at 9 AM and closes at 11 PM.

* **Metropolitan Museum of Art** – At 1000 Fifth Avenue, and locally simply known as the Met, this is one of the greatest museums of fine arts in the Western Hemisphere. It is open Sunday thru Thursday from 10 AM to 5:30 PM, and from 10 AM to 9 PM on Friday and Saturday.

It is said to be the third most visited museum in the world, and it is one of those must see venues in the city.

* **Museum of Modern Art** – Known as MoMA, it is located at 11 West 53rd Street in midtown. The museum is considered to be the quintessential museum for viewing modern or contemporary art, and is without question one of the world's largest. Even the architectural style of the building is in keeping with the modern tradition. If you are not appreciative of modern art then my suggestion would be not to visit.

Hours for visiting are Monday thru Thursday from 10:30 AM to 5:30 PM, Friday remaining open until 8 PM. Weekend hours are also from 10:30 AM to 5:30 PM.

* **National 911 Memorial & Museum** – Now one of the greatest attractions of the city, it is located in Westfield World Trade Center at 180 Greenwich Street. The memorial is essentially hallowed ground, as it occupies the exact site where the twin towers destroyed on September 11th, 2001 stood. There is a somber, yet warm feeling to the site. Yes it evokes the memories of the tragedy, but it is a fitting symbol of national resilience. The museum houses many artifacts from the original World Trade Center, including fragments of the former buildings. You must obtain tickets in advance because of the popularity of this amazing tribute.

Visit *www.911memorial.org* for information and to purchase tickets. Hours are 7:30 AM to 9 PM for the memorial and the museum is open Sunday thru

Thursday from 9 AM to 8 PM, remaining open until 9 PM on Friday and Saturday. I would say that a visit should be high on the agenda of every visitor who remembers that fateful day.

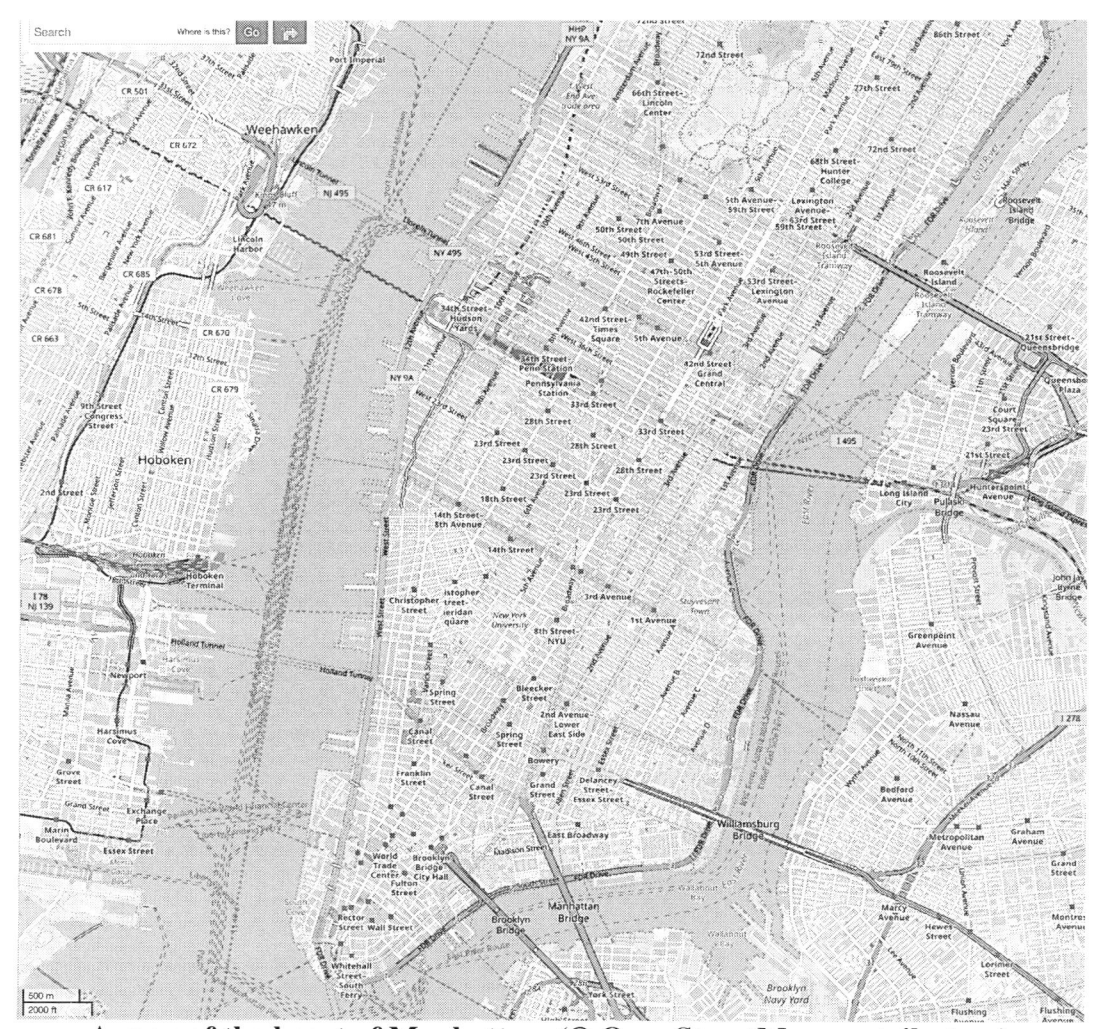

A map of the heart of Manhattan, (© OpenStreetMap contributors)

* **One World Observatory** – For a dramatic view from the 100th to the 102nd floors of One World Trade Center, this is another one of those must see venues when visiting the city. On a clear day you will be able to see north along the Hudson River, northeast into Connecticut and east across much of Long Island. The view west is over New Jersey. Again this is a venue where tickets are a must in advance. Visit *www.oneworldobservatory.com* for full details and ticket purchase.

A view looking to midtown Manhattan from One World Trade Center, (work of Beyond my Ken, CC BY SA 4.0, Wikimedia.org)

* **Rockefeller Center** – This is a venerable complex at 45 Rockefeller Plaza in midtown Manhattan is one of the most recognized sights in the city. Its famous plaza houses an ice skating rink in winter and the city's beloved giant Christmas tree. The center plaza is open 24/7, but various venues have their own respective times. Visit the web pages at *www.rockefellercenter.com* for a directory of facilities, their hours of service along with news of special events at the time of your visit.

* **Statue of Liberty** – The most iconic of New York City monuments, this great lady stands on its own small island close to the New Jersey shore. To reach the statue, you must take a ferry from Battery Park in lower Manhattan, which also stops at Ellis Island. From the New Jersey shore you can take a ferry from Liberty State Park at the Railroad Terminal.

It is open daily from 8:30 AM to 4 PM and is administered by the National Park Service. All Golden Passport cards are honored for admission. Visit on line at www.statueoflibertytickets.com/Statue-of-Liberty.

Looking south at Times Square – the most typical daytime view

* **Times Square** – There is no other crossroads in the United States as famous as that where 42nd Street crosses Broadway, known as Times Square. This is the heart of the entertainment district and it is famous for its blazing neon signs and rather gaudy advertising displays.

Times Square has its competitors, Piccadilly Circus in London and the Ginza in Tokyo as well as Fremont Street in Las Vegas. But in the end, there is only one Times Square. This is also the heart of the theater district where most of the on and off Broadway theaters are located. Whenever you visit, it is crowded with people and traffic, and you need to be careful and keep up your guard against pickpockets, especially after dark.

ACCOMMODATIONS: There are more fine hotels in New York City than possibly any other city in the world. I am only recommending what I consider to be the best four and five-star properties in Manhattan since you do not want to be too far from the cruise terminal either for departure or upon arrival due to traffic congestion. Hotels in New York City are expensive even in the three and four-star categories, so you might as well spend a tad bit more and stay at one of the best the city has to offer. All of the hotels in my selected listing offer full in house dining and room service. Also consult your cruise line, as many have special pre or post cruise arrangements with major hotels and can offer you a group rate. Here are my personalized choices for excellent hotels shown alphabetically:

* **Conrad New York** – A Hilton property at 102 North End Avenue, this is a very distinctive hotel with a modern vibe that carries through the guest and public rooms. There is full service dining, a fitness center and meeting facilities. Its rates are competitive and well below those of other properties of equal quality. I GIVE IT ****

* **Crowne Plaza HY36 Midtown Manhattan** – Well located at 320 West 36th Street, close to shopping, entertainment and all midtown venues. Guest rooms are nicely appointed. The dining facilities and other services are comparable to those of much higher priced properties. There is both a fitness and business center on site. This is a mid-level hotel that is sure to please those on a budget. I GIVE IT ***

* **Crowne Plaza Times Square Manhattan** – Well located at 1605 Broadway, this more moderately priced hotel in the heart of the entertainment district offers nice rooms, fine dining and all the services of a major hotel. The hotel offers a fitness center and meeting rooms. It is convenient for both business and pleasure travelers and is so close to many of the most popular venues. I GIVE IT ***

* **Evelyn Hotel** – An Art Deco property at 7 East 27th Street, this is a very affordable, yet comfortable hotel with style and a real touch of class. The guest rooms and all services are very good and the tariffs are well within affordable limits. There is a main dining room, a pastry shop and lounge. And there is a fitness center. I GIVE IT ***

Four Seasons Hotel

* **Four Seasons Hotel New York** – A superb member of the illustrious Canadian hotel chain, this is the prime Four Seasons for New York City. It is located at 57 East 57th Street with prime views of Central Park. Like all Four Seasons properties, the guest rooms are exceptionally tasteful, the dining facilities and all guest services are impeccable and provide for the finest in quality. I GIVE IT *****

* **Four Seasons Hotel New York Downtown** – At 27 Barclay Street, this lower Manhattan Four Seasons offers all the elegance and luxury of its sister hotel in midtown. The guest rooms, dining facilities and guest services are all superb and meet the highest standards in this smaller property. The hotel offers a full service spa and indoor pool. It is in the heart of the financial district and convenient for business executives who have meetings in this area. I GIVE IT *****

* **Langham New York Fifth Avenue** – A venerable name at 400 5th Avenue, this is an outstanding hotel offering elegance at a more reasonable rate than the five-star names. The style of the hotel leans more to the modern side, but without compromising its level of posh quality. The hotel has a spa and fitness center. I GIVE IT ****

* **Loews Regency New York** – Located at 540 Park Avenue, this is a very excellent hotel with beautiful guest rooms, an outstanding restaurant and lounge, a fitness center and spa and all the added touches of an upmarket property. I GIVE IT ****

* **One Hotel Central Park** – A very fine quality hotel at 1414 6th Avenue, this boutique hotel offers Old World elegance with a modern vibe at a price that is quite reasonable for the level of service and dining. The guest rooms are modern, yet have a definite European vibe. There is a fitness center and meeting facilities. I GIVE IT ****

* **Park Hyatt New York** – Located near Central Park at 153 West 57th Avenue, this is Hyatt Hotel's best New York properties. A very fine hotel with class, elegance and superb service being that it is one of the top line Hyatt properties. There is a fitness center and pool, and a full service business center. This more contemporary hotel offers all of the elegance and dignity but at a price that is more in keeping with other major top line hotel brands. I GIVE IT *****

* **Peninsula Hotel** – A noted hotel facing Central Park at 700 5th Avenue, this hotel, part of the famous Hong Kong group, offers the finest in luxury and elegance in every aspect of its presentation. Guest rooms and suites, dining and all services are at the top of the chart when it comes to quality. The hotel has a full service spa, fitness center and pool. And as is true for all of New York's best hotels, the daily tariff is quite high. Many cruise passengers, especially sailing with the five-star lines also want the same level of luxury during their stay in the city. Here you will definitely find the best of the best. I GIVE IT *****

* **Pierre** – A well-known elegant property at 2 East 61st Street at the corner of 5th Avenue, today it is part of the magnificent Taj Hotel group. The Pierre is a very posh and Old World style hotel with superb accommodation, two dining rooms, afternoon tea service and offers all the services one expects from a world class hotel. Once again, this is an expensive property, but it is a real treat if you are willing to splurge. The Pierre is a Four Seasons property. I GIVE IT *****

The Pierre Hotel

* **Plaza Hotel** – There is probably no more famous name for a New York hotel than the Plaza. Located at 768 5th Avenue at the southern margin of Central Park, this hotel has housed more famous people than any other. Anyone who read stories by Kay Thompson about Eloise and her exploits will recognize this hotel. And in the family history of President Trump, he once owned the hotel and gave it to his first wife Ivana as part of their divorce settlement. The Plaza is elegant and expensive. Its guest rooms and suites are plush and the service is impeccable. The dining rooms are known for their quality of food and service. I have enjoyed many happy hours at the Plaza. If you can afford it, why not. I GIVE IT *****

The Plaza Hotel from Central Park

* **Ritz Carlton New York** – At 50 Central Park South, this luxurious hotel offers the finest in comfort and luxury. The rooms and suites are elegant, the dining and lounge facilities are especially plush and apart from daily meals, afternoon tea is served. There is a fitness center and pool. A full service spa is on site. This is a superb hotel for its services and location. I GIVE IT *****

DINING OUT: It is very difficult to describe the dining potentials in New York City. To be concise, the number and diversity of restaurants and bistros is almost endless. And prices range from ultra-expensive to very reasonable to downright cheap given all the food carts and trucks that abound. If I were considering New York City as one of the ports of call on the cruise, I would need to offer pages of dining experiences. But for those of you who are planning to spend some pre or post cruise time, I am offering up just a handful of my personal favorites. I will not mention any of the restaurants in the hotels I have recommended, but wish to note that all my hotel choices were in part based upon the quality of their dining rooms. Here alphabetically is a short list of my all-time favorites. Consider this to be purely a personal list, as it omits hundreds of fine restaurants for the sake of expedience since New York City is not an actual cruise destination. Here are my choices shown alphabetically:

* **Broadway Bagel** – At 2658 Broadway, this is a very popular restaurant that is casual, informal and simply fun. They do specializes in bagels and other quality breads and pastries. Sandwiches, omelets, pancakes, wraps and other American favorites are served for breakfast and lunch. And they offer a wide array of fresh baked dessert items. They are open daily from 6 AM to 8 PM. Reservations are not necessary.

* **Capital Grille** – This popular eatery is found at 120 West 51st Street. It offers up a diverse menu that includes seafood, grilled meats and also vegetarian dishes. And it is also noted for its cheesecake on the dessert menu. The atmosphere and service are both quite good. They are open weekdays from 11:30 AM to 9 PM, weekends from 5 to 9 PM. Call ahead for a table at 212 245 0154.

* **Club A Steakhouse** – For meat lovers you will be pleased with this selection at 240 East 5th Street. Steak is the featured theme, but other grilled meats, chops, poultry and seafood are on the full service menu that starts with appetizers, soups and salads. The quality of the food and service along with a pleasant atmosphere make for a good experience. Hours are from 5 to 10 PM Monday thru Saturday. Call 212 688 4190 to book a table.

* **Estiatorio Milos** – Located at 125 West 55th Street, this Mediterranean seafood restaurant offers up the bounty of the sea, served with a very strong Greek accent. Freshness and traditional methods of preparation assure you of a superb meal complimented by appropriate wines. You will find dishes from the Mediterranean that other seafood restaurants are not prepared to serve. Their hours are daily from 11:30 AM to 8:30 PM. Call them at 212 245 7400 to book.

* **Gallagher's Steakhouse** – At 228 West 52nd Street, this is a top quality steakhouse that serves a full menu with appetizers, a raw bar, salads, soups and an array of steak, chops, poultry and seafood. Atmosphere, food and service are all superb, as is their selection of wines. They are open weekdays from Noon to 10 PM and weekends from 5 to 10 PM. Reservations are advised, call 214 586 5000 to book.

* **Jacob's Pickles** – Located at 509 Amsterdam Avenue, this somewhat eclectic eatery offers up traditional American dishes with a New York twist. Portions are large and there is quite a selection of entrees that they show as

"home cooking," and these are typically comfort food. There are dishes from New England, the South and the Southwest along with basics you would find in the Midwest. Long hours enable you to dine at your leisure. Weekday hours are from 10 AM to 10:30 PM and weekend hours are from 9 AM to 10:30 PM. Reservations are not needed.

* **Mei Jin Ramen** – This superb Japanese restaurant is found on the upper east side at 1574 2nd Avenue. Specializing in ramen along with a variety of other traditional Japanese dishes, they are sure to please. Their hours are from Noon to 3 PM daily and 5 to 10:30 PM weekdays. Call ahead at 212 327 2800 for reservations.

* **Napkin Burger Hell's Kitchen** – Located at 630 9th Avenue, this popular and typical American restaurant features great hamburgers, vegetable and chicken burgers, great fries and very good desserts in the old fashion tradition. They are open daily from 11:30 AM to 10 PM and you can call 212 757 2277 to book your table.

* **Obas** – Located midtown at 647 9th Avenue, this excellent Thai, Vietnamese restaurant presents outstanding dishes in an authentic manner, served in a dining room filled with ambiance. Cuisine and Atmosphere combine with great service. They are open daily from 11:30 AM to 11 PM with extended dining to Midnight Friday and Saturday. Call 212 245 8880 for reservations.

* **Ocean Prime** – At 123 West 52nd Street, this is a very popular restaurant in midtown that serves very hearty meals. Seafood is high on their list, as are steaks and chops, accompanied by a significant wine list. Hours are Tuesday thru Thursday from 11:30 AM to 9 PM and Friday thru Monday from 4 to 9 PM. Call them at 212 956 1404 to book a table for dinner.

* **Piccola Cucina Osteria** For excellent Chinese cuisine in the heart of downtown, visit them at 196 Spring Street in Soho. Here you will find a diverse but traditional menu with an emphasis upon the Neapolitan tradition. Their hours are from 11:30 AM to 11 PM daily with extended closing at Midnight Friday and Saturday. Call 646478 7488 for reservations.

* **Sotocasa Pizzeria** – If you are a fan of great New York style pizza then it is worth a trip over to Brooklyn where you will find them at 298 Atlantic Avenue. Their pizza and other very Italian dishes will please without doubt. They are open from 5 to 11:30 PM weekdays and from Noon to 11:30 PM weekends. Call 718 852 8758 to reserve your table.

SHOPPING: New York City is one of the greatest cities in which to shop for just about anything you can desire. Prices and quality vary from the very cheap to the ultra-expensive. I will not go into great detail, as there are so many shopping guides published for the city. I simply will point out a few important venues.

Department store shopping would include four major named stores that are worth visiting if for no other reason than to window shop. These stores are:

* **Bergdorf Goodman** is located at 754 5th Avenue for their women's store and at 745 for the men's store. This upmarket name is related to Neiman Marcus of Dallas, Texas.

* **Bloomingdale's** flagship store is located at 1000 3rd Avenue. It is an upmarket store comparable to Neiman Marcus.

* **Macy's** flagship store at 34th Street and Broadway, the largest single department store in the country, possibly in the world.

* **Saks and Company** has their flagship store at 611 5th Avenue, a name that is comparable to Bergdorf Goodman.

The most elegant street for overall shopping is 5th Avenue where you will find many great names. It is an experience to simply walk the avenue and window shop if you are not seriously looking to buy. I could fill pages with the brand name stores that are found along this fashionable street.

FINAL WORDS: In closing this chapter, all that needs to be said is that New York City is almost legendary in the minds of those who visit. There is so much to offer that visitors become mesmerized by the city and they tend to overlook the crowding, congested living standards, high cost of living, relatively high crime rate and the many neighborhoods that are impoverished. This no doubt can be said for many world class cities, but in New York City these conditions are quite significant. Yet they are pushed aside by most visitors.

LESS FREQUENTED NEW ENGLAND PORTS OF CALL

Map of the New England coast, (© OpenStreetMap contributors)

Depending upon the itinerary of your cruise, you may or may not visit one or more of the less frequented ports of call along the New England coast. The ones most likely to be included, if at all, are (from north to south):

* **Rockland, Maine** is located north of Portland. It is a small town on a deeply indented bay that lives primarily for fishing with lobster being the prized catch. Rockland gives you a chance to explore a small Maine port.

* **Bar Harbor, Maine** can be the first or last American port of call depending upon your itinerary. It is a resort community on Mount Desert Island and is home to Acadia National Park, the most northeasterly of the national park system.

* **Martha's Vineyard, Massachusetts** is an island located off the Cape Cod Peninsula south of Boston. It has a long history dating to colonial times when whaling was an important activity. Today it is a resort island that primarily caters to a very wealthy segment of the population.

* **Newport, Rhode Island** is a city with a long colonial history that also became home to the wealthiest of New York tycoons during the late 19th century when they built what were called summer cottages, but which were in fact great mansions that emulated those of British aristocracy.

Lobster fishermen hard at work in Maine waters off Rockland

The following chapters will cover each of these four less frequented ports of call. As noted above, there could still be other lesser visited ports of call, especially on the itineraries of the smaller, luxury ships or those in the adventure class. However, having searched itineraries for the prior two years I did not come across any that I felt would merit attention other than the ones to be covered in the remaining chapters of this book. There are many small villages along the coast of Maine, but there is nothing special about them that would warrant adding them to an itinerary, especially with regard to the type of activities these more specialized cruises are based upon. Adventure cruising in the New England-Eastern Canada market is thus quite limited, as the majority of people who enjoy this itinerary in the fall are generally retired or semi-retired and no seeking out the more rigorous adventure itineraries.

The rugged coast of Maine is more like that of Nova Scotia than the other New England states

BAR HARBOR, MAINE

Map of Bar Harbor and Acadia National Park, Maine
(© OpenStreetMap contributors)

Many cruise ships travel between Halifax, Nova Scotia or St. John, New Brunswick and Portland, Maine overnight, therefore missing the natural beauty of the area around Bar Harbor - Acadia National Park on Mount Desert Island. For those that do include a stop in Bar Harbor, consider yourselves lucky to visit one of the most popular New England destinations among those who motor around the region, especially in the fall.

THE PHYSICAL SETTING: A stop at Mount Desert Island off the northeast coast of Maine is a treat for those who love natural beauty, especially during the fall color season. When seen from out at sea, the highest peak of the island appears to be desert like because it is above timberline and is rather barren. It was French explorer Samuel de Champlain who first used that designation when describing the higher mountaintops. Once you approach the island, you quickly see that it is in no way a desert. Just the opposite is true. This rugged island that was once heavily glaciated is covered in thick mixed forests of pine and broadleaf deciduous trees.

The island is especially scenic. Although the highest peak only reaches 465 meters or 1,528 feet above sea level, it remains bare because of the nature of its hard rock core and the on shore gale force winds that can blow during the winter season. It is the combination of the hard granitic rock and the winter gales that limit the growth of trees at the highest altitudes.

When full color arrives to Acadia National Park

The total area of the island is 279 square kilometers or 108 square miles. With its two major mountain peaks, there are numerous small glacial lakes and streams that feed down to the coast, giving the island the feeling of being much larger. Although there are deposits of sediments, the core of the island is ancient granite over 500 million years old. And this granite has been quarried since the 19th century in many parts of Maine and New Hampshire, and today with interior home design favoring granite for countertops and flooring, the industry continues. New Hampshire is actually nicknamed "The Granite State" but instead it is referred to as the "Pine Tree State." Glaciation helped expose more of the island's three granitic cores, ultimately making it easier for quarries to be developed. Fortunately today most of the island has national park status, thus the most of the land is now protected so quarries are no longer active here.

Being on the coast, the summer weather is generally cool, and occasional fogs do linger. The cool weather and beautiful scenery attracted many people from Boston and New York City, purchasing summer homes around the island. The dramatic scenery also tantalized many noted artists, and there is still a demand for both realistic and impressionistic paintings from this area. And many artists have chosen to make the island home. However with Acadia National Park occupying a good portion of the island, future expansion of vacation properties is more limited.

Winter can be quite severe because of exposure to the open Atlantic. Heavy snows or a snow and rain mix will alternate throughout the winter. Thus few visitors come during the winter months, preferring the less stormy interior of New Hampshire and Vermont where skiing has become a major attraction.

A BRIEF LOCAL HISTORY: At present less than 10,000 people are permanent residents of the island, with 5,300 living in the popular tourist resort of Bar Harbor. Before the coming of Europeans, the Wabanaki natives used the island during summer to gather berries, collect clams and hunt for game.

The first European to arrive was Samuel de Champlain who ran aground in 1604 and had to then set about repairing his ship. But although this was part of what ultimately became French Acadia, no settlement was made until after the British had secured it in the treaty that ended the French and Indian War in 1763. Thus there is no French heritage on Mt. Desert Island.

What is today Bar Harbor was incorporated in 1796, but its early economy was based upon lumber, fishing and shipbuilding along with limited agriculture. It was not until the mid-19th century that city residents from Boston and New York began to recognize the resort potential of the island, this inspired by several of the Hudson River School artists whose works depicted the landscape with great appeal. By the late 1880's, there were numerous hotels and private summer residences around the shores of Bar Harbor. Ultimately rail and ferry service made the island very accessible and it became one of the most fashionable places to spend the summer, the other being Newport, Rhode Island. One of the best-known families to vacation here was the very wealthy Rockefeller family. The Astor and Vanderbilt families also had homes in Bar Harbor as well as in Newport, Rhode Island.

In 1947, the state of Maine experienced a very dry summer, sparking wildfires across the state. By the fall, conditions had deteriorated, and on Mount Desert Island a massive fire burned into November, consuming dozens of grand vacation homes, five of the resort hotels and nearly 200 smaller homes. Fortunately the town center and many of the early Colonial homes were spared, but over 10,000 acres of beautiful forest burned. This in many ways put an end to the so-called Golden Age of great wealth in Bar Harbor. Today it is a popular vacation destination, but no longer the playground of the super-rich. Much of the land devastated by the fire has slowly regenerated, as it has been 70 years since that fateful blaze.

Today most of the island is preserved by the federal government as Acadia National Park, one of the few national parks in the eastern portion of the United States. The park consists of the bulk of the mountainous terrain and includes numerous glacial lakes, bays and coves thus presenting some of the most tranquil costal scenery in all of New England.

CRUISE SHIP TENDERS: The town of Bar Harbor does not have any harbor facilities capable of handling even the smaller luxury cruise ships. Thus all cruise ships must anchor off shore in deeper water and tender their guests to and from shore. The small dock where tenders land is within easy walking distance of the town center.

THE PHYSICAL LAYOUT OF THE PORT: Bar Harbor is a very small town that is built on a small bulge in the island that gently slopes upward from the water. Highway 3 enters the town from the north then makes a sharp turn to the east and a few blocks later another sharp turn to the south. This southern portion is the main commercial street. There are only a few square blocks in central Bar Harbor covering less than one square kilometer. The rest of the town spreads into the lower hills on a series of curvilinear streets.

The predominant building material is wood and the style is that of colonial New England, giving Bar Harbor a sense of great visual appeal. Many small guest houses and inns stretch along Highway 3 on both sides of the town, as inland the land rises quickly into forest land, much of it preserved within the boundaries of Acadia National Park.

WHAT TO SEE AND DO: Your ship will no doubt spend a full day in Bar Harbor. There are no true port facilities and thus Bar Harbor cannot handle most cruise ships, as passengers are tendered on shore, which on the very large ships can be a slow process. This is a blessing in disguise, as it prevents the town and the island in general from becoming overrun by thousands of ship passengers at any one time, but it is inconvenient for passengers. This is one factor that keeps the mega cruise ships from including Bar Harbor in their fall itineraries.

A map of Bar Harbor, (© OpenStreetMap contributors)

You have two options as to sightseeing. You can spend the day in Bar Harbor, but there is not much to see outside of the small downtown and historic core. Your best action is to plan on visiting Acadia National Park, which covers the major portion of the island. To accomplish this these are the options open to you:

* **Ship sponsored tours** – Your cruise line will sponsor motor coach tours around the island that focus primarily upon Acadia National Park. If your visit is at the time of peak fall color then by all means you should take either a group or private tour through the park. And some cruise lines also offer walking tours of Bar Harbor.

Looking down upon Bar Harbor (Work of Idawriter, CC BY 3.0, Wikimedia.org)

* **A car and driver** can be arranged by your cruise ship's shore concierge desk. This is the most expensive way to see the island, but it gives you total control over your day. You may also wish to visit on line with Acadia Magic with regard to private touring. Visit www.acadiamagic.com/tours for details.

* **Rental cars** are available, but they can also be relatively expensive. Then you have the responsibility of driving, which is less enjoyable for the person who drives.

* **Hop on hop off trolley** – There is a sightseeing trolley that takes guests from Bar Harbor through Acadia National Park with stops where you can get off, explore and then take the next trolley. For further details visit their web pages at www.olliestrolley.com .

MAJOR SIGHTS TO SEE: Here are the major attractions that I believe should not be missed (shown alphabetically)

* **Abbe House** – In Bar Harbor at 26 Mount Desert Street, this museum is specifically dedicated to the history and artifacts of the Native-American people who once inhabited the state of Maine. The museum is open daily from 10 AM to 5 Pm through October.

The fall beauty of Acadia, (Work of Jeff Gunn, CC BY SA 2.0, Wikimedia.org)

* **Acadia National Park** - Whether by tour coach provided through your cruise line, private car with a driver/guide or by taxi or trolley, you should take the standard drive through Acadia National Park to enjoy the magnificent fall scenery. If you are on a group tour, the stops at points of interest will be predetermined. If you have the flexibility of a car or taxi, you can enjoy the sights at your leisure. If you are an American resident and have what is called a national park Golden Passport, there will be no admission charge to enter the park. If you do not have a pass, there is an entrance fee, as is true with all national parks.

* **George B. Dorr Museum of Natural History** – Downtown Bar Harbor at 105 Eden Street, this museum is dedicated to the interpretation of the natural history of coastal Maine, including its significant marine life. The museum is open Tuesday thru Saturday from 10 AM to 5 PM.

* **Mt. Desert Street and the Village Green** - Again if you remain in town, you can take a walk along the main shopping and dining street and visit the Village Green, typical of the old town commons found throughout New England

Jordan Pond within the park is a serene spot

* **Ocean Path** - Just south of Bar Harbor is the Ocean Path, a walking trail that follows the rugged coastline through some beautiful scenery along Frenchman Bay. The head of the path can be accessed from the town either on foot, by bicycle or taxi.

* **Shore Path in Bar Harbor** - If you choose to remain in town, you can start at the town pier and walk along the shoreline of the island, pass beautiful homes and guesthouses and enjoy a bit of nature without leaving the town area.

DINING OUT: As a tourist oriented destination, there are more restaurants in Bar Harbor for the size of the community than would otherwise be normal. Many cater almost totally to tourists and summer residents. Most visitors are looking for lobster, as after all this is Maine. The level of quality varies, not freshness because that is something you cannot escape. My recommendations are for those few restaurants that are both open for lunch and offer top quality, and this is very limiting since most of the good restaurants are only open in the evening. My choices are limited, as the majority of the excellent dining establishments are not open for lunch and as a cruise ship passenger you will not be here for dinner:

The main shopping and dining area of Bar Harbor (Work of Adavyd, CC BY SA 3.0, Wikimedia.org)

* **C-Ray Lobster** – At 882 State Highway 3, this restaurant features the freshest seafood, with Maine lobster being a featured item on the menu. Steamers are also a featured menu item, as is the grilled cheese and lobster sandwich. Fresh seafood chowders are another favorite. Their hours are from 11 AM to 8 PM daily.

* **Galyn's** – Located at 17 Main Street, this is a popular seafood restaurant in which bisques, chowders and soups are a specialty. And of course lobster is a prominent menu item. Meat lovers and vegetarians are not forgotten, as there are menu items for them, but seafood rules. They are open daily from 11 AM to 9 PM. Call to see if you need a reservation at 207 288 4855.

* **Jordan's Restaurant** - Located in town at 80 Cottage Street, Jordan's is only open for breakfast and lunch, closing at 2 PM. It has a good lunch menu, typically American, but it does feature fresh seafood. Reservations are not necessary.

* **Peekytoe Provisions** – Located at 244 Main Street, fresh seafood and seafood chowders dominate the menu, and of course lobster is king along with crab cakes and fish. They also do have vegetarian options. Hours are 11 AM t 7 PM Wednesday thru Saturday and 11 AM to 5 PM Sunday. You can check if reservations are needed at 207 801 9161.

* **Side Street Cafe** - 49 Rodick Street in the town center, this is a popular deli type establishment that serves sandwiches, lobster rolls and complete hot entrees including whole lobster. It is one of the few recognized restaurants that is open for lunch. They are open from 11 AM to 9 PM weekdays and close at 10 PM Friday and Saturday. Reservations are not necessary.

* **The Stadium** – At 62 Main Street, this popular place for lunch. They have a menu that features lobster rolls, whole lobster and other local seafood dishes. And their pies and cookies are excellent. They have a local reputation for great cheesecake. Hours of service are between 9 AM and 9 PM daily and reservations are not necessary.

* **West Street Cafe** - At 76 West Street, it is open starting from 11 AM. The restaurant is rather basic with very non-descript decor, and the menu is also rather basic, but the quality is good and they offer daily luncheon specials, nothing fancy, but essentially good. They are open from 11 AM to 8:30 PM daily with extended closing at 9 PM Friday and Saturday. Reservations are not necessary.

SHOPPING: Bar Harbor is a tourist community and thus its main streets are filled with a great variety of gift shops and boutiques. Most of what is sold has little or nothing to do with Mount Desert Island or the State of Maine. You can buy everything from gourmet foods to books, Christmas ornaments and clothes. I have not been in any shops that were specifically oriented to local arts and crafts, but there are several galleries featuring noted artists whose works are relatively expensive.

FINAL NOTES: Bar Harbor is highly commercialized, none of the glamor and elegance of its Golden Age remains. I get the feeling today that most establishments are simply there to make money, but that may just be a personal observation. It is the scenery of Acadia National Park that is the gem, and if the weather is good, you will not be disappointed in the landscape. That is what initially drew in people back in the 19th century and what made Bar Harbor popular.

ROCKLAND, MAINE

Map of Rockland, Maine, (© OpenStreetMap.com)

Rockland, Maine is the least visited of the ports of call in the New England portion of any fall color cruise itinerary. Less than 40 cruise ships will stop at this rather picturesque small Maine town despite the good reviews given by guests to the cruise lines. There is not much to see or do in Rockland, but it is the ambiance of this small coastal lobster fishing port that is why ship guests seem to appreciate. You may find Rockland listed as a port of call on a two-week itinerary from the more upmarket cruise lines and rarely see it listed on

an itinerary for the major cruise lines operating large ships. Yet for people visiting coastal Maine during the summer and fall on their own, usually driving their own vehicle, this is one of those very quaint small towns that people find so captivating.

THE NATURAL LANDSCAPE: The surrounding landscape is one of a very irregular coastline marked by dozens of small bays and offshore islands reflecting the impact of ancient glacial action. The hard granite rock does erode slowly and leaves a visual landscape of steep hills pockmarked by ponds and lakes and a rugged coastline where the surf breaks in dramatic fashion. Thus small bays became havens for fishermen when they recognized the bounty of the sea.

The land around Rockland is heavily forested, primarily in pine with willow and other deciduous trees that add splashes of color in the fall when they prepare for dormancy. Fog is one of the natural elements of the Maine coast that has been a problem for fishermen during summer and fall and it is then that you hear the fog horns up and down the coast. The lighthouse became a manmade feature of the Maine coast to guide sailors along its coasts. Winter is cold and blustery and snowfall can be quite heavy. This is not a season when visitors would willingly choose to visit the Maine coast.

The Rockland waterfront emerges from an October fog

A BRIEF ROCKLAND HISTORY: Although Rockland is known for its lobster, cod and haddock fishing, it began as a lumber town when in 1767 three brothers created a camp to be able to exploit the pine and oak to produce staves used in storing salted fish and also in the ageing of alcoholic spirits. The pine was used by shipbuilders, especially for masts. By the mid 1800's fine sailing ships were built in Rockland.

Deposits of lime were found outside of Rockland and this added to the potential for the growth of the community. There are still remnants of the old lime quarries outside of Rockland. In the 19th century lime was an important product for use in interior plastering. At its height Rockland was a major producer of lime, and there was a fair amount of exploitation of the surrounding countryside with over 100 kilns in operation processing the raw material. Rockland produced around one million casks of finished lime. By the 1950's the quarried were silent, as the entire interior finishing industry switched to more synthetic materials. Today a few of the old lime kilns have been preserved on the National Registry of Historic Places.

An old postcard showing the busy docks of Rockland in the late 1800's

In 1871 the opening of a rail link to the outside world made it easier for Rockland to ship out both its casks of lime, but it also brought in visitors to enjoy its beautiful coastline, as people living in Boston and New York began to venture out on holidays, a new economic potential. And even today visitors still come, especially during the fall color season. Only today's visitor comes from much greater distances. Hotels and inns began to spring up with the Samoset Hotel becoming the mainstay of the tourist trade after first opening in 1889. The old hotel is long gone, destroyed by fire, but there is a more modern Samoset Resort that still is the featured player in Rockland's tourist traffic.

The Rockland waterfront, (Work of Crispins C Crispain, CC BY SA 4.0, Wikimedia.org)

The name Rockland may not be not be a household word, but this small town still has quite a following among people living in the northeastern part of the country. It is still a place where summer and fall visitors bring in a lot of revenue for the economy, competing with fishing, especially for lobster. And Rockland has been pictured in calendars with its flaming fall colors and beautiful Victorian mansions.

SHIP TENDER SERVICE: The docks at Rockland are not capable of handling even a small cruise ship. Thus ships drop anchor in Penobscot Bay and then tender their guests to and from the shore. Once on the shore, the heart of town is accessible with less than a five minute walk. And if a cruise line is offering any motor coach tours, there is room for the coaches or private cars to be waiting.

The historic main street of Rockland, (Work of Crispins C. Crispian, CC BY SA 4.0, Wikimedia.org)

The Knox County Courthouse, (Work of Doug Kerr, CC BY SA 2.0, Wikimedia.org)

WHAT TO SEE AND DO: Rockland does not have a sizeable infrastructure to handle ship passengers in great numbers. Thus the large cruise ships do not often call in at Rockland.

There are fewer options available in this port than most of the other locations on cruise itineraries. The options open include:

* **Ship sponsored tours** – Many cruise lines do not offer motor coach tours in Rockland, but for those that do, the tours will generally be confined to the local area. And some cruise lines may offer a walking tour of the town since it is rich in historic Victorian architecture.

* **Private car and driver** – Most cruise lines can arrange for a private car and driver, but this service is somewhat limited so you need to book early if this is your preference. You may also with Best Limo to see what they offer. Visit on line at www.bestlimodb.com/CityServices/ServiceArea=Rockland.

* **Trolley Service** – There is a trolley service in Rockland that operates during the summer season, but it may not be operating in mid to late fall. Visit www.camdenrockland.com/businesses/all-aboard-trolley for details.

* **Taxi touring** -is possible. Simply negotiate a tour with any taxi you find available and the drivers know the town well and act as good guides.

* **Walking** is also an enjoyable way to tour Rockland in nice weather. Much of the town can be seen on foot for those who are capable.

SIGHTS TO BE SEEN: There are a few distinctive venues in Rockland that are worthy of note. They are listed here alphabetically:

* **Farnsworth Art Museum** – This small museum is worth a visit, as it contains numerous paintings by many New England artists, most notable being Andrew Wyeth. The museum is open from 10 AM to 4 PM Wednesday thru Sunday and is located at 16 Museum Street.

* **Rockland Breakwater and Lighthouse** – There is a long breakwater that gives added protection to the shoreline and the fishing boats moored alongside. Penobscot Bay is rather open to storm surges and the breakwater, which was built in the 19th century offers the needed protection. It is 1,200 meters of 4,000 feet in length. The lighthouse is open to visitors daily between 10 AM and 5 PM.

The small Rockland Lighthouse at the far end of the breakwater

* **Rockland Harbor Trail** – This is a five mile long path that follows the Rockland waterfront. In the town center there is a section of just over half a mile long that is hard surface and the remainder is gravel, but still easy to walk.

* **Rockland Historic District:** During the 19th century there was a significant influx of summer visitors of means. As a result, Rockland saw the construction of many fine homes built in the Victorian style. Earlier homes built during the first part of the 19th century also reflect the typical New England colonial style of architecture.

On a fair weather day you can enjoy strolling the streets of Rockland's older neighborhoods and enjoying these beautiful homes. These historic homes are considered the pride of Rockland.

Some cruise lines may offer a walking tour of the older part of Rockland, which can be quite rewarding to anyone interested in historic architecture.

A fine example of Rockland's Victorian mansions, (Work of Crispians C. Crispin, CC BY SA 4.0, Wikimedia.org)

DINING: For those who wish to sample some great seafood, and in particular fresh lobster there are a few good restaurants open during the lunch hour. I call your attention to the following:

* **Archer's on the Pier** – At 58 Ocean Street right on the waterfront, this is a popular and well-patronized restaurant in which the fresh seafood, and in particular lobster dominates the menu. Their menu also features a few vegetarian dishes. Open daily from 11 AM to 9:30 PM with 10 PM closing on Friday and Saturday, reservations are not necessary.

* **Brass Company Café** – At 305 Main Street, here you will find massive sandwiches featuring seafood, in particular lobster served with fresh coleslaw and fries. They also offer vegetarian dishes. Service is daily from 5 AM to 3 PM and reservations are not needed.

* **Hill's Seafood Company** – Located at 266 Main Street in the heart of Rockland, this a popular luncheon spot for fresh seafood, and in particular for

lobster rolls, a local tradition. They are open daily from 11:30 AM to 9 PM and reservations are not necessary.

* **Rockland Café & Bakery** – Located at 441 Main Street, this restaurant is known for its fresh soups, chowders and fish and chips. Service hours are from 5:30 AM to 9 PM daily and reservations are not necessary.

You know your seafood is fresh in Rockland, as you watch the fishermen bringing in their catch

SHOPPING: The small downtown features several gift shops and boutiques and you will find a selection of handmade items, as quilting and wood carving are longtime Maine traditions. By the middle of fall many of the small shops keep abbreviated hours, but will generally be open when a ship is anchored in the bay.

FINAL WORDS: Rockland always received high marks in evaluations given by ship guests, not for anything spectacular, but rather for its unique charm. This is a quintessential Maine coastal town that presents itself well.

MARTHA'S VINEYARD, MASSACHUSETTS

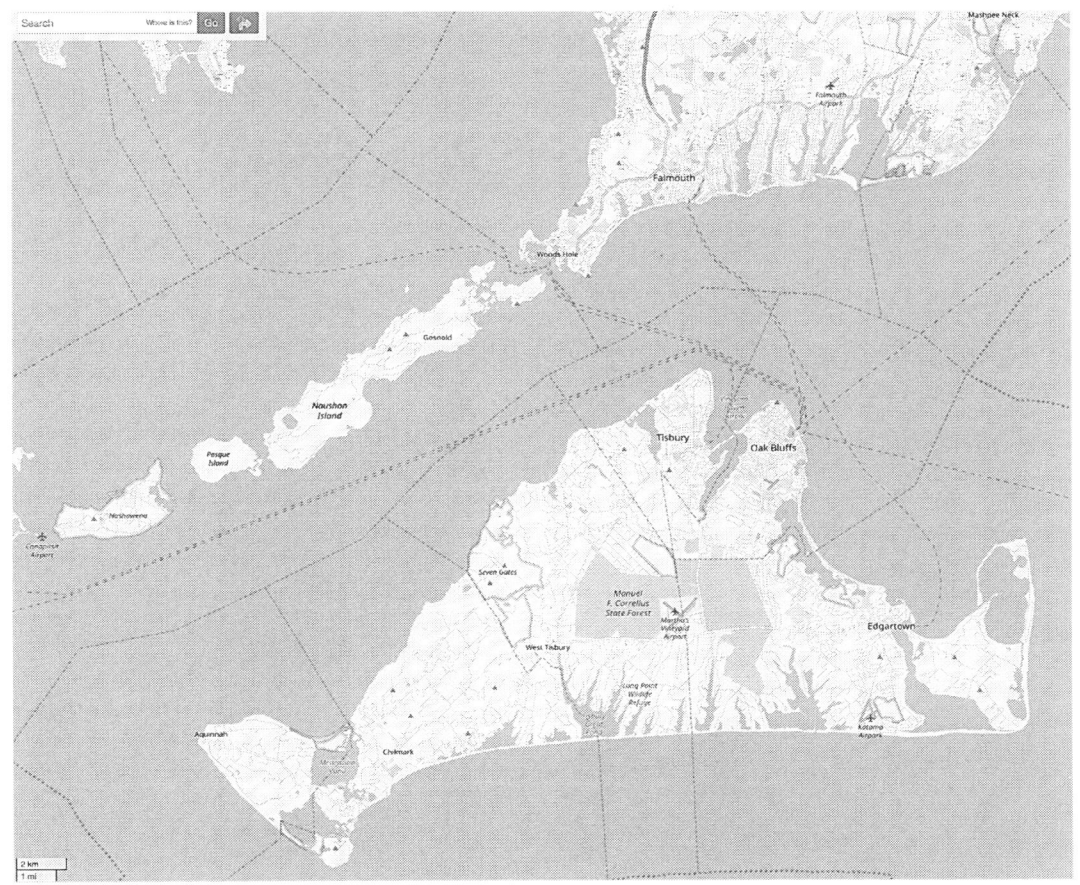

Martha's Vineyard in relation to the mainland (© OpenStreetMap contributors)

Martha's Vineyard and Nantucket are two small islands off the south coast of Massachusetts, and a part of the state. They are both popular summer resorts and have famous reputations for their graceful way of life. Martha's Vineyard is the larger of the two with a total land area of 87.5 square miles or 226 square kilometers , including the smaller adjacent island of Chappaquiddick, which is connected by a small bridge because the distance is only a few meters or feet. If that name seems familiar to American readers, it is because of the automobile accident that the late Massachusetts Senator Ted Kennedy had in 1969 in which a young lady died. These are low lying islands composed of glacial deposits, the maximum elevation being only 311 feet or 95 meters above sea level. The permanent population is approximately 17,000 residents, but that number grows by tens of thousands during the summer season.

Of the two islands, when cruise ships do visit, it is to Martha's Vineyard rather than Nantucket. And even the schedule for Martha's Vineyard is quite light since the vast majority of major cruise lines call in at Newport, Rhode Island if anywhere between Boston and New York City.

THE GEOGRAPHIC SETTING: Glacial moraines formed both Martha's Vineyard and Nantucket during the last glacial retreat that ended around 10,000 years ago. As the glaciers stagnated during their retreat, they deposited ridges of mixed boulders, sand and mud, which solidified, being high enough to still remain as islands when the sea began to rise. The islands are relatively flat to just gently rolling, and the highest points of land are the tops of the moraine ridges. The shores are low lying and there are numerous small bays and offshore sandbars. The vegetation cover varies from mixed coniferous and broadleaf deciduous woodlands to marshes and grasslands.

Chappaqiddick Island typifies the landscape of Martha's Vineyard, (Work of Arwcheek, CC BY SA 4.0, Wikimedia.org)

These two islands sit in the open ocean, though Martha's Vineyard is very close to the mainland. Summer weather will vary from warm to occasionally hot, and humid. Winter can be very blustery, as storms track up from the southwest, often bringing gale force winds. And on rare occasions, tropical hurricanes can get this far north and bring much destruction and flooding. Snowfall in winter is moderate, depending upon the overall severity of the season.

Martha's Vineyard contains numerous small coastal towns and villages, and summer homes are scattered all around the island's edges, as this is still a very special playground for the wealthy, and especially for those in high-ranking government. The Kennedy Family has spent much time on the island, and Jackie Kennedy lived here part time until her passing. And in 1999, John Kennedy, Jr. his wife and sister-in-law were killed in a small plane crash just offshore, as they were coming for a family wedding. During and after Bill Clinton's presidency, the Clintons have frequented as well. The first president to have visited while in office was Ulysses Grant. The most recent presidential visit was in 2009, when the Obama family spent its vacation on Martha's Vineyard.

ISLAND HISTORY: When visiting Martha's Vineyard, it is helpful to know in advance much of the history of the island, as it figures so much into what you see in the landscape and is also a fascinating look at the nation's wealthy and powerful social leaders as well. To this day the cost of living on the island averages 60% higher than the national average, a good key as to its cultural makeup. Likewise the cost of housing is almost double the national average.

There is still some question as to the name of the island, but it has been ascribed to British explorer Bartholomew Gosnold who named a smaller island Martha's Vineyard when he sailed by in 1602. Much later the name was given to the larger island that bears it today. But what it had to do with the raising of vines is still not clear. The name is one of the oldest continuing place names in the nation, and interestingly it is one of only five that has an apostrophe in its spelling.

Thomas Mayhew from Watertown, Massachusetts purchased the rights to the island from British owners, and Mayhew's son was the first to settle in 1642. His son befriended one of the Wampanoaga tribe who lived on the island and thanks to that friendship many of the natives converted to Christianity. Ultimately one of the Wampanoaga would graduate from Harvard University. And many Wampanoaga still live on the island today, their lifestyle interwoven with the rest of the population. Mayhew's son was drowned on a voyage to England, but his grandsons continued to administer to the small colony. The island reverted to the Duke of York, but was put under the jurisdiction of the

Colony of New York in 1671, and the Mayhews became the chief administrators.

In 1683, Martha's Vineyard was incorporated as part of Dukes County, New York, but in 1691 it was transferred back to Massachusetts.

It was the whaling industry that figured so prominently in the 19th century history of both Martha's Vineyard and Nantucket. This was an era of great prosperity, but also of many tragedies, as ships often met their doom in this dangerous business. And the goal was primarily to bring back oil, which was used as lighting fuel for early American homes. But by the 1870's, the industry met its demise with the advent of kerosene made from petroleum. But by this time, people of means were traveling farther from home during the summer months, and with a railroad and boat connection through Woods Hole, the influx of summer residents and visitors began to fill the void left by the collapse of the whaling industry.

Into the 20th century, the island gained even greater fame as a playground for the very wealthy, but also it became a holiday resort for those of the middle class. In 1974, millions came to know the island in the movie *Jaws, Jaws 2* and *Jaws: The Revenge* since much of the filming took place in two of the island villages.

CRUISE SHIP DOCK OR TENDER: When cruise ships visit Martha's Vineyard they will either dock or tender guests ashore at Oak Bluffs, which is one of the two major settlements when looking at it along with Vineyard Haven as the most populated hub. Oak Bluffs is located on the northeastern coast and can accommodate only small size cruise ships at its dock. The majority of cruise ships normally tender their guests ashore. A few small cruise ships will call into Edgartown, the main island community, but this would also require a tender service.

WHAT TO SEE AND DO: The island is quite small and for its size it is sprinkled with vacation homes and there is nothing much else to see in the way of historic venues. Much of what you will see is very tourist oriented, but the architectural treasures are those houses and public buildings that date back to the 18th and 19th centuries. The options for sightseeing include:

* **Organized ship tours** – the best way to see the island is to take one of the group coach tours offered by your cruise line. The fall season on the island is relatively quiet, as most summer vacationers and residents have left. The motor coach tour will give you a good overall view of the island.

* **Small groups** may be best off using Martha's Vineyards Tours & Excursions to arrange for more semi-private sightseeing. Check out their web page at *www.marthasvineyardexcursions.com*

* **Private car and driver** may be difficult to arrange as private cars with driver/guides are few in number. Most of the major sights are around Edgartown, the island's main community and thus an organized tour is your best option.

* **Local taxi tours** – This option of using a taxi is not as successful as elsewhere on the cruise since there are few in service on the island.

* **VTA Bus** – There is a public bus service operating called the Vineyard transit Authority. When you arrive at the dock or tender port there will be maps showing the routes of the local bus. For $6.00 you can buy an all-day ticket, which is quite convenient. During the fall the bus service is scaled back and depending upon when your ship arrives, it may not be all that convenient.

PLACES TO VISIT: My recommendations for must see sights include the following list shown alphabetically:

The glacial moraine cliffs at Aquinnah on the west end of the island

* **Aquinnah Cliffs** - In Aquinnah, these cliffs represent the more elevated glacial moraine, as it skirts along the seashore presenting a very picturesque landscape, showing that the island is varied geographically.

* **Circuit Avenue** - The main street of Oak Bluffs is a great place for a stroll or to window shop.

* **Edgartown Lighthouse** - Located along the Edgartown Harbor, this lighthouse museum is one of three operated today by the Martha's Vineyard Museum. It was once very important in the days of the whaling ships. It is open 10 AM to 5 PM seasonally.

* **Gay Head Lighthouse** - Located in Aquinnah on the other side of the island, this was also a very important lighthouse in its day. It too is operated by the Martha's Vineyard Museum and open from 11 AM to 4 PM seasonally.

* **Martha's Vineyard Camp Meeting Association** - Located in the heart of Oak Bluffs at 80 Trinity Park, this amazing collection of brightly painted Victorian cottages is part of what was once a Methodist meeting camp for summer activities. It is one of the best examples of Victorian cottage architecture in New England.

* **Mytoi** - A beautifully designed Japanese garden that is very beautiful and tranquil, located on Dike Road, Chappaquiddick Island. There is a definite serenity to this tiny bit of Japan located here on this New England island.

* **South Beach** - Along the Edgartown waterfront, this is a quiet and very picturesque beach backed up by rows of sand dunes.

DINING OUT: Most of the good island restaurants are only open for dinner, and this cuts down the number of possibilities for lunch, especially as the season ends in early October. Depending upon the date of your fall cruise, you may end up visiting when the island is heading toward its dormant season. I am listing just a small number of restaurants in the upper tier that are open for lunch in the early offseason. The restaurants listed below are those open for lunch that I consider to be the best of the island. Most are not in Edgartown, thus if you ship tenders off shore here, you will need to take a taxi to the majority of the restaurants. My choices are shown alphabetically below:

* **Larsen's Fish Market** - Located at 56 Basin Road, Dutcher's Dock in Menemsha, and open from 10 AM to 7 PM, this is an outstanding restaurant

for the freshest seafood dishes. One of their specialties is lobster mac and cheese. You will not need a reservation.

* **Martha's Vineyard Chowder Company** - In Oak Bluffs at 9 Oak Bluffs Avenue, this is a great place to visit if you really love seafood chowders. They also offer fresh salads and hot entrees, but you will find that a hearty bowl of chowder alone is quite filling. They are open from 10 AM to 10 PM daily with 11 PM closing on Friday and Saturday. Reservations are advised. Call them at 508 696 3000 to book a table.

* **Menemsha Fish Market** - Located at 54 Basin Road, Dutcher's Dock in Menemsha, this excellent seafood restaurant is one the few good establishments open for lunch. Their seafood chowder, lobster bisque, fresh fish and lobster make it worth taking a taxi from Edgartown. They are open daily from 10 AM to 5:30 PM but with 11:30 AM opening on Sunday. Call 508 645 2282 to ask if you need a reservation.

* Net Result - In Tisbury at the Marketplace, this is another excellent restaurant for fresh seafood, open Monday thru Saturday from 9 AM to 6 PM. They serve outstanding crab cakes and chowders, among many other dishes. You will not need a reservation.

SHOPPING: The same holds true for Martha's Vineyard as I noted for Bar Harbor. This is a destination where the shops cater to visitors and summer residents, offering all types of goods, specialty foods and some antiques, but nothing representative of the island or its culture. Therefore I do not have any shops to recommend. There are shops located on the main streets of Edgartown and Oak Bluff.

FINAL NOTES: Martha's Vineyard is a quaint and beautiful island, once home to the super rich, but today available to a larger audience. Located closer to the mainland dock, it is in such close proximity as to have become the more heavily patronized than Nantucket.

It is hard to see much of the island in a single day. The areas where the ships dock are more heavily populated, and it is hard to see the real charm and tranquility of the island.

NEWPORT, RHODE ISLAND

The core area of Rhode Island (© OpenStreetMap contributors)

Rhode Island is the smallest of the 50 states, its total land area of 3,144 square kilometers or 1,214 square miles is less than one third the size of the physical area of Juneau, capital city of Alaska. As one of the original 13 British Colonies, Rhode Island has a long and very rich history. Its two major cities of Providence and Newport are architecturally distinctive in that they have retained much of the colonial flavor despite being modern cities. The heart of the state is Narragansett Bay, which gives the state over 482 kilometers or 300

miles of shoreline despite only being 53 kilometers or 37 miles in width. When you drive through Rhode Island from the border of Connecticut and through Providence into Massachusetts, it only takes about an hour depending upon traffic.

THE NATURAL SETTING OF RHODE ISLAND: The state is primarily coastal plain, with a few hills rising in the north, but to only a maximum elevation of just over 243 meters or 800 feet. There are still vestiges of the original mixed broadleaf deciduous forest cover in the north, but most of Rhode Island is today devoted to farmland and urbanization.

The most important feature of the state is Narragansett Bay, which creates a massive indentation into Rhode Island. Numerous significant islands break up the uniformity of the bay, thus giving it an overall appearance as being much larger in total area than its water surface alone would create. The bay is what attracted early settlers and the fertile islands and margins made Rhode Island a good place in which to settle.

Sailing into Newport Harbor from Narragansett Bay

A BRIEF HISTORY: Newport is quite old, dating back to 1639 having been settled by religious dissidents from Portsmouth, Rhode Island and the

Massachusetts Bay Colony. Most turned to the Baptist faith, forming their own congregation. But even within the colony there were two factions that did not see eye to eye on spiritual matters. None the less, the community did grow and it became the dominant town in the colony. Adding to the cultural fabric were immigrant Spanish and Portuguese Jews fleeing the Spanish Inquisition in 1658 along with Jews that had fled the former Dutch colony of Recife in Brazil, driven out by the Portuguese Catholics. They formed first synagogue congregation in the American Colonies followed later by the one in Savannah, Georgia. A second influx of Jews from Portugal during the mid 1700's ushered in much of the trade and commercial activity that would propel Newport into the ranks of major ports in the colonies. One of the immigrants introduced the trade in whale oil and this not only became a major manufactured product, but it also brought about a fleet of whalers similar to the ones from Nantucket and Martha's Vineyard.

By 1663, the Rhode Island colonies received a Royal Charter as a unified colony and Benedict Arnold became its first governor. The Old Colony House was completed in 1741 and served as the colonial building and later state house until 1904 when Providence became the only state capital rather than sharing the role with Newport.

At the time of the American Revolutionary War, Newport was not only a successful whaling port, center for processing the oil and an important trade port, but it also became known for fine furniture production. During the Revolutionary War, the British at one point captured Newport in order to protect their hold on the harbor in New York. In 1778, the colonial forces, aided by the French, ultimately took back Rhode Island, but could not capture Newport. Fortunately in 1780, the British consolidated their forces in New York, simply abandoning their position in Newport.

In addition to legitimate activities, Newport also saw its share of pirates using the port, and the city also was involved with the slave trade on an indirect basis. Sugar from the Caribbean was distilled into rum in Newport, the rum then taken to West Africa where it was used to buy slaves that were brought to the Caribbean Islands or the southern colonies, this despite a state law in 1787 prohibiting such trade that was passed shortly after American independence.

The Revolutionary War had crippled Newport economically and the city essentially became a shadow of its former greatness until the 1840's, when initially southern plantation owners began to establish summer homes on the coast, but it was by the 1870's, that wealthy industrialists from the mid-Atlantic region began to develop what would become recognized as the palaces of Newport. Each wealthy industrial or trade family tried to outdo the other, and

Newport saw the most extravagant displays of wealth seen anywhere in the country. Not only did they build such grand mansions, but also they developed a summer social scene like no other. This grandeur lasted until the Great Depression, which did cripple many of the very rich, but others survived. However, following the Depression and World War II, the so-called Gilded Age of Newport was over. Today most of the mansions are either museums or are used for private schools and other civic institutions.

Fort Adams guarded Newport well after the American Revolutionary War, started in 1821

Newport does have an important place in the world of yacht racing, especially the prestigious Americas Cup, with more races having been held off Newport than any other city in the competition. However, in recent decades American yachtsmen have not been as successful in winning the cup and therefore Newport has not hosted the race in some time. It is of course dependent upon the country of the host port to win the prior year's cup.

CRUISE SHIP TENDER SERVICE: The harbor at Newport is only capable of handling pleasure craft. It has no docks sufficient in size to accommodate even a small cruise ship. However, the dock at Fort Adams is capable of handling small cruise ships. This dock is located within the fortress grounds and then requires a shuttle bus to ferry guests into the town center. Most cruise ships that visit Newport are of medium or large size and therefore they must anchor in Narragansett Bay and tender their guests to a small landing inside the pleasure craft harbor. The procedure takes half an hour and is somewhat inconvenient, but at least guests are in the heart of the city and can then board their tour coaches, private cars, taxis or go of on their own. There are no terminal facilities at either location.

Expensive yachts in Newport Harbor

THE PHYSICAL LAYOUT OF NEWPORT: Present day Newport has a population of approximately 25,000 residents. In addition to being a colonial city with a rich architectural tradition, it is also a city that became recognized in the late 19th century for its palatial mansions built along the coastal drive at the southern tip of the island. These grand summer homes became some of the most celebrated lavish homes in the nation, reflecting the great wealth of the families that had the built. And in many ways they rivaled the palaces of Europe, which the wealthy industrialists tried to emulate.

The city of Newport is located on Narragansett Bay on Aquidneck Island, connected to the mainland by several bridges. The island, like the rest of the state, is relatively flat with only a few small hills. There is virtually no natural landscape on Aquidneck Island, as it is nearly all urbanized, but with Newport and its suburban towns under bowers of trees.

The island is relatively long and narrow, and its southernmost margin reaches the open Atlantic. The southern portion of the island narrows into a rocky peninsula that rises higher than the rest of the land. Here the shoreline is rocky with waves crashing along its margins. This area had not been developed, as it was not deemed desirable to the colonial city. But when the wealthy elite began to see places for their mansions, this became choice real estate because of its dramatic heights and superb views over the open sea.

The island has a marine climate in which summer weather is cool to balmy, but on occasion does get quite warm and humid. But generally there is always a nice breeze blowing in from the open ocean. And fog is not uncommon during the summer. Winter can be very cold, blustery and at times especially difficult to contend with. There are periods when heavy snowfall occurs, especially during very cold winters. The autumn colors come late because of the temperate conditions that persist into late October, and they are not nearly as brilliant as inland locations.

In addition to its colonial charm with a large number of buildings from the pre-revolutionary era and great mansions, the city is home to Salve Regina University, the United States Naval War College and the Naval Undersea Warfare Center.

WHAT TO SEE AND DO: The majority of ships must anchor off shore and tender passengers on shore, a process that does consume some of the time allocated for this port call. The tenders bring passengers to the main yacht harbor adjacent to the historic city center. Given the configuration of the harbor, it takes an average of 30 minutes to come ashore. The time consumed in tendering is what keeps the large and mega size cruise ships from visiting Newport. It would be a monumental task for them to bring passengers onshore and return them to the ship in a timely manner.

HOW TO TOUR NEWPORT: There are so many historic sites to visit in Newport, and a number of distinctive historic districts that it is impossible to get to develop a true feeling for the city during a one-day port call. As much as I always prefer and recommend having independence in your ability to tour, Newport is one of those ports where a half-day guided tour gives you the best overall impression. Then you can use the remainder of the day to get around the central city on your own, thus combining both aspects of exploration.

* **Ship sponsored tours** - Most cruise lines offer walking or coach tours to enable you to see the major highlights of the city. And these tours often include one or more of the great 19th century mansions in which the admission and provision of a guide are already taken care of for you.

* **Private car and driver** - A car and driver/guide or a prearranged rental car through one of the major agencies enable you to sightsee on your own. But unless it is arranged in advance, you do loose valuable time in securing the hired car. Your best option, although more costly, is to have a private car and driver.

You may also wish to check with Tours by Locals at their web page to see what they can offer. Contact www.toursbylocals.com/Newport-Tours .

Another source to check is Tour and Guide by visiting their web page at www.tourandguide.com . You can then compare prices and services.

* **Semi private touring** - Narrated tours of the city are offered by Viking Tours of Newport. For details as to their services, visit *www.vikingtoursnewport.com* where you can also book.

* **Hop on Hop Off bus touring** - The hop on hop off trolley is a simple way to get around the cliff drive where the great Newport mansions are to be found, but you then must make your own arrangements to visit the interior of at least one or two to garner the full experience. Check the web page at *www.tourservicesnewport.com* for schedules, routes and fares.

* **Taxi touring** - Taxi drivers are usually waiting at the tender drop off and offer their services on an hourly or flat fee basis for sightseeing. The drivers are very knowledgeable of the city and its history.

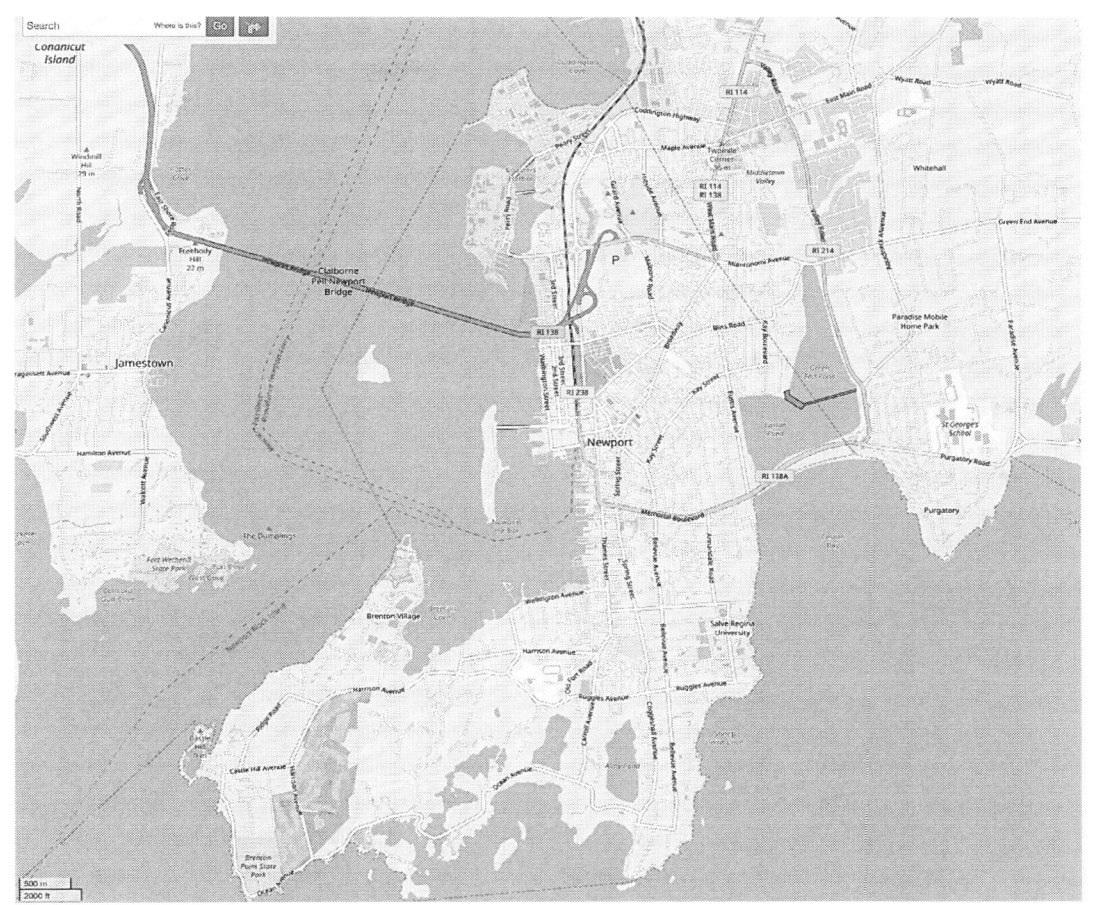

A map of central Newport, (© OpenStreetMap contributors)

* **Walking tours** - Walking around the historic old part of the city is relatively easy when you get off the ship's tender, but it is too far a distance to visit any of the grand 19th century mansions. You will need a taxi or the hop on hop off trolley to get out to the tip of the peninsula to see these grand palaces.

THE MAJOR SIGHTS: Here are my recommendations of the most important highlights during a one-day port visit to Newport, shown alphabetically:

* **Bellevue Avenue** - This is the in city part of the Ocean Drive where you will see a great number of the mansions of the rich and famous that date back to the Gilded Era of Newport. A car, taxi or tour coach is needed, although if you are a good walker, it is possible to stroll this street, which ultimately will take you past the Marble House and The Elms with The Breakers being just a few blocks east.

* **Bowen's Wharf** - This is the old waterfront wharf dating to the years when Newport was a major colonial trade center. Today many restaurants and boutiques are located around the wharf, making it focal to tourism in Newport. The wharf is adjacent to the dock where the cruise ship tenders tie up.

* **Breakers** - This is the ultimate largest and grandest of the Newport mansions, once the summer retreat of the Vanderbilt family. If you tour only one mansion, it should be this one, which many ship tours do include. It is located at 44 Ochre Point Avenue and open daily from 9 AM to 5 PM. You will need to take a taxi or the hop on hop off trolley to get here.

The Breakers main drive (Work of Upstate NYer CC BY SA 3.0, Wikimedia.org)

* **Cliff Walk** - This is a 5.6 kilometer or 3.5-mile long walkway that runs along the cliffs at the south end of the island where many of the great mansions are located. It is especially nice on a clear day and you will get incredible views of The Breakers, which is the most famous of the Newport mansions. To get to the walk you will need a car, taxi or the hop on hop off trolley. But your ship's tours may include this activity as part of one tour selection. Once you start along this walk, there is no place in which to end your excursion until you reach the other end, so be prepared to walk the entire distance.

* **Fort Adams State Park** - The fort is a massive stone citadel whose inner courtyard is home to the Newport Jazz Festival each year. This was the colonial era fort that protected the approach to the city from the sea. It is open from 6 AM to 9 PM daily. Guided tours are given between Noon and 2 PM weekdays and between 10 AM and 3 PM on weekends.

* **Marble House** - At 596 Bellevue Avenue, this is the second greatest and most elaborate mansion built in the 1880's for the William Vanderbilt family before they commissioned the building of The Breakers. Hours are 10 AM to 5 PM daily.

* **Ocean Drive** - This is the complete very scenic tour around the southern end of the island, noted for its magnificent scenery and the elegant mansions, especially on a nice and clear day. Once again, a car, taxi or tour is required to engage in this activity.

A map of the heart of Newport

* **Thames Street** - Running parallel to the old waterfront, Thames Street is the main commercial and dining street for old Newport's downtown. It is lined with many buildings that date back to early colonial times.

* **Trinity Church** – There is a simplicity to Trinity Church that speaks to the conservatism of early New England. The stereotypic New England church seen on calendars is always white and has a slender dominant steeple. This church looks as if it was consecrated yesterday and yet has three centuries behind it. It was founded in 1698 but the building only dates to 1724 and is a beautiful structure. Visitors are welcome Tuesday thru Friday from 10 AM to 2 PM. The church is at 1 Queen Anne Square.

Trinity Church just before Halloween

* **Truro Synagogue** - Located in the Washington District at 50-52 Spring Street, this is the oldest synagogue in the United States, founded in 1763. It is open from 9:30 AM to 2:30 PM with tours every half hour from 10 AM to 1:30 PM. There are no visitations permitted on Jewish holidays.

* **Washington District** is one of the oldest parts of Newport and it is located just to the north of the tender drop off point in the small yacht harbor. Washington Square is the main public square of the city and it is the focus of

this historic district that contains many of the oldest and best preserved of the city's colonial architecture. At one time during the Colonial Era what is now called the Washington District was the core of Old Newport. It will give you a good feeling for the nature of the city during its early years when Newport was one of the most important New England towns, yet there was never any great extravagance given that there was strong religious conservatism. The Golden Era for Newport actually came from wealthy outsiders in the 19th century.

Historic Washington Square

There are many more individual mansions and old colonial houses to see in Newport, but to concentrate effort on individual buildings means you will lose sight of the entire feel for the city. Thus I have not mentioned the dozens of houses, colonial public buildings and churches that are found throughout the city center with some of them open for public visits. It is more to your advantage to divide your time between the major mansions along the Ocean Walk, the old downtown district and the Washington District along with several of the intervening residential streets to gain an overall feeling for the flavor of Newport. Keep in mind that Newport offers two faces, the most important being its Colonial Era history and the other being found on the Ocean Walk where the great mansions of wealthy 19th century industrialists were built.

Spring Street in the historic Washington District

DINING OUT:
As with so many ports of call, you will only have time for lunch while in Newport, which rules out a majority of the truly fine restaurants. The majority of those open for lunch are rather typically American and do not offer much of the New England flair people often want. Of course seafood does figure prominently on most menus. My recommendations are for those with as much of the New England flair as possible, and likewise only those open for lunch:

* **Annie's** – In town at 176 Bellevue, this is a typical Newport eatery serving great breakfasts including corned beef hash, lunch soups, salads and sandwiches along with fresh fish and chips. They also offer lobster salad as a lunch specialty. They do serve vegetarian dishes. They are open Thursday thru Monday from 7 AM to 2 PM for breakfast and lunch. Reservations are not required.

* **Brick Alley Pub** – Located at 140 Thames Street, this is a good old fashioned New England restaurant with great food. They specialize in seafood fresh from the Atlantic, and lobster figures prominently. They make great soups, mac and cheese, chowders, sandwiches and pizza. They are open Monday thru Saturday from 11:30 AM to 9 PM, remaining open until 9:30 PM

Friday and Saturday. Sunday hours return to 9 PM closing. Reservations are not required.

* **Castle Hill Dining Room** - At 590 Ocean Drive inside the Castle Hill Inn, this is a very typical New England Inn restaurant. It is open from 5:45 to 9 PM and has a varied menu to please any taste. They also have an afternoon High Tea that is very typically British, but if your ship departs around 5 PM it will be impossible to attend the tea. Call 888 466 1355 to check on their tea time or to book a table if your ship is staying late.

* **Corner Café** - At 110 Broadway, this is a very popular establishment with locals. It is Monday thru Wednesday from 7 AM 2:30 PM and remain open until 9:30 PM Thursday thru Saturday. Sunday hours are from 7 AM to 4 PM. Call 401 846 0606 to book a table. Most locals and visitors love it for breakfast. They serve typical American comfort food, but well prepared.

* **Mooring Seafood Kitchen** - At 1 Sayer on the waterfront, this is a seafood restaurant with the chowder, fish and lobster dishes you expect in New England. And one of their lunch specialties are lobster rolls. Cod, haddock and clams are also featured. They are open from Noon to 8 PM daily. Call 401 846 2260 to see if you need a reservation.

* **Stoneacre Pantry** - At 515 Thames Street in the city center, this is an especially fine quality restaurant that prides itself in using local ingredients that are uniquely prepared. Their soups, poultry, fish and other entrees are excellent and they receive glowing reviews from local food critics. Their serving hours are from 5 to 8 PM Monday thru Thursday, remaining open until 9 PM Friday. On Saturday they serve from 9 AM to 9 PM and on Sunday from 9 AM to 8 PM. Call 401 619 7810 for reservations.

SHOPPING: There are so many small shops and boutiques in Newport that cater to the summer residents and tourists that it would be impossible to name even a dozen or more. But like Martha's Vineyard and Bar Harbor, few will have local crafts available, but rather they will be selling overpriced clothing, jewelry, ceramic and glassware, antiques and other collectibles that for the most part do not really reflect the heritage of Newport. They cater to those visitors who have the impulse to buy just because they are on vacation. And of course there are so many shops selling the normal tourist kitsch such as T-shirts, post cards, magnets and the like. These are the main areas to shop:

* **Bowen's Wharf** - The old commercial waterfront dock area that is today a very popular destination for those wanting to visit fine quality shops and boutiques. Shops on the wharf are open Monday thru Saturday from 10 AM to 5 PM and Sunday from Noon to 5 PM.

* **Thames Street** - The main shopping street of Newport, parallel to the old harbor front is loaded with small shops and boutiques.

Thames Street in the old downtown

* **Bannister's Wharf** - Just north of Bowen's Wharf, this is another similar shopping venue. Shops have different hours, but essentially most are open at 10 AM and remain open into the early evening.

* **Brick Marketplace** - Between Thames Street and Americas Cup Avenue, this is the former city market. There are three rows of small stalls and shops selling a variety of gift items, and it is here where you will find a few handmade items by local craftsmen. Shops are open daily from 9 AM to 6 PM.

* **Long Wharf Mall** is a one block pedestrian mall just north of the tender drop off point. It is lined with numerous boutiques and several name brand

clothing stores. Hours of service vary with each merchant, but essentially the shops are open from 9 AM to 6 PM daily.

Long Wharf Mall leading to Washington Square

FINAL WORDS: Newport is a city that offers more in the way of history and a variety of architectural styles from early colonial to the height of Victorian elegance, but it offers more than can be seen during a one-day port call. It is not the kind of a destination that is really best suited for seeing while on a cruise. But hopefully it will whet your appetite to make a return visit on your own. There is enough to keep you occupied for a couple of days.

ABOUT THE AUTHOR

Dr. Lew Deitch

I am proud to say that I share dual nationality and citizenship with Canada and the United States and I am a semi-retired professor of geography with over 46 years of teaching experience. During my distinguished career, I directed the Honors Program at Northern Arizona University and developed many programs relating to the study of contemporary world affairs. I am an honors graduate of The University of California, Los Angeles, earned my Master of Arts at The University of Arizona and completed my doctorate in geography at The University of New England in Australia. I am a globetrotter, having visited 97 countries on all continents except Antarctica. My primary focus is upon human landscapes, especially such topics as local architecture, foods, clothing and folk music. I am also a student of world politics and conflict.

I enjoy being in front of an audience, and have spoken to thousands of people at civic and professional organizations. I have been lecturing on board ships for a major five star cruise line since 2008. I love to introduce people to exciting new places both by means of presenting vividly illustrated talks and through serving as a tour consultant for ports of call. I am also an avid writer, and for years I have written my own text books used in my university classes. Now I have turned my attention to writing travel companions, books that will introduce you to the country you are visiting, but not serving as a touring book like the major guides you find in all of the bookstores.

I also love languages, and my skills include a conversational knowledge of German, Russian and Spanish.

I presently live just outside of Phoenix in the beautiful resort city of Scottsdale and still offer a few courses for the local community colleges when I am at home.

**TO CONTACT ME, PLEASE CHECK OUT MY WEB PAGE
FOR MORE INFORMATION AT:**
http://www.doctorlew.com

Made in United States
Troutdale, OR
08/17/2023